# Mormonism:

## What Does the Evidence and Testimony Reveal?

Dr. John M. Oakes
with Douglas Jacoby

# Mormonism:

## What Does the Evidence and Testimony Reveal?

**Mormonism: What Does the Evidence and Testimony Reveal?**



Printed in the United States of America.

ISBN: 978-1-939086-03-7



Cover and book interior design: Toney Mulhollan.

A special thanks to Amy Morgan for her editorial contributions.

John Oakes is a professor of chemistry at Grossmont College. John became a Christian while attending graduate school in 1978. He earned a Ph.D. in chemical physics in 1984 from the University of Colorado. That same year he married his wife, Jan. They have three adult children and reside in San Diego, California. John also serves as president of the Apologetics Research Society. Some of his other books include: *Is There A God?*, *From Shadow to Reality*, *Reasons for Belief*, *Daniel: Prophet to the Nations*, *That You May Believe*, *Field Manual for Christian Apologetics* and *The Christian Story: Finding the Church in Church History*. For more information about John's ministry work, go to www.EvidenceForChristianity.org.

Dr. Douglas Jacoby graduated in 1980 from Duke University (history). In 1982, he received an MTS from Harvard (New Testament), followed by three years of post-graduate study at Kings College London. He took his doctorate in 1999 from Drew University (Christian Education). In addition to serving as Adjunct Professor at Lincoln Christian University, Douglas has had an international teaching impact for several decades, preaching in 500 cities in over 100 nations around the globe. For addtional information about his ministry, visit www.DouglasJacoby.com and www.jacobypremium.com.

Illumination Publishers International
www.ipibooks.com
6010 Pinecreek Ridge Court
Spring, Texas 77379-2513

# Contents

# Introduction

"Joseph Smith is a prophet and the Book of Mormon is the Word of God. This is my testimony and I know it in my heart. I pray that one day you, too, will experience what I have experienced." Many of us have heard this opening line, or something very similar to it. A lot can be learned about a person or group of believers from their opening introduction. This is certainly true with the Church of Jesus Christ of Latter-day Saints, more commonly known as the Mormons.

What is the history of this group that according to its own statistics, has grown from 1 million in 1957 to 14.5 million today? What are their beliefs? Where are they coming from, and why has the group experienced such astounding success, against formidable odds?

This book will address all these questions in detail, but let us begin by analyzing the Mormon testimony. We can see from the outset three things that are absolutely essential to understanding their beliefs. The three keys to understanding the Mormon movement are:

1. The life, character and ministry of Joseph Smith.
2. The Book of Mormon, the supposed "second Testament of Jesus Christ."
3. The emotional/experiential testimony of the followers of Joseph Smith.

At its heart, the Mormon religion is about a feeling—a "burning in the heart." The essence of the appeal of the Latter-day Saints is personal testimony. It is not the intellectual appeal and certainly not the historical accuracy of Smith's writings. Neither is it rational argument or appeal to the worldly or materialistic.

For a number of years I had the mistaken belief that, in essence, the Mormon movement is similar to the Jehovah Witnesses. Both began with cult-like tendencies and followed a charismatic leader. Both made Jesus something less than God. Both rely on an efficient, hierarchical system to maintain order within their communities. Both work principally through local ministries, not a professional ecclesiastical staff. Both have grown steadily and rapidly through an unstinting emphasis on evangelism. Only recently did my friend Glenn Giles, a Bible teacher in Denver, point out the profound difference between the underlying appeal of these two groups. The parallels listed above are real, but the similarity is deceiving. Whereas the essence of Mormonism is an emotional/experiential appeal to the heart, the central nature of the Jehovah Witness appeal is intellectual. It is about argument, human logic and rational proof: The followers of the Russellite movement are right and everyone else is wrong. Think of it this way: Mormonism is to Jehovah's Witnesses as heart is to mind.

The order of the keys to understanding Mormonism listed above is significant. The first key to unlocking the mystery of Mormonism is to understand the life of the founder, chief apostle and prophet of Mormonism, Joseph Smith, one of the most fascinating figures in American history.

Joseph Fielding Smith, one of the former presidents of the LDS church and a direct descendant of Joseph Smith, clarifies:

> Mormonism... must stand or fall on the story of Joseph Smith. He was either a prophet of God, divinely called, properly appointed and commissioned, or he was one of the biggest frauds this world has ever known. There is no middle ground. If Joseph Smith was a deceiver, who willfully attempted to mislead the people, then he should be exposed; his claims should be refuted, and his doctrines shown to be false.[1]

Smith's analysis is valid. For this reason, we will begin with a detailed study of the life, character and methodology of Joseph Smith, as we try to understand why thousands were willing to leave everything behind, face withering persecution, and follow him across several states.

Only after plumbing the depths of the man can we begin to analyze the Book of Mormon. Without this book, there would be no Church of Jesus Christ of Latter-day Saints. What is its story? What doctrines does it teach? What are its marks of inspiration, if any? Why is it that so many believe it is, in fact, a "second testament of Jesus Christ"?

From there we will proceed to explore the bizarre doctrines found, not so much in the Book of Mormon, but in the doctrinal and theological works of Joseph Smith, Brigham Young, and others, which appear in *Doctrine and Covenants* and *The Pearl of Great Price*. Having reached a basic understanding of the scripture of Mormonism, we will proceed to explain the organization of the present-day Utah Mormon movement and its evangelistic methods, followed by suggestions for how to reach out to members of this group and bring them to a more correct knowledge of Jesus Christ.

What is it about the life of the Utah Mormon Church, that makes their testimony so powerful, and what can we do to help those involved in this movement to find their way to an accurate understanding of the gospel of Christ? Probably for most who read this volume, the main reason for doing so is in order to answer this question. We hope you will not be disappointed.[2]

# Chapter 1

# The Early Life of Joseph Smith[3]

Joseph Smith was born in Sharon, Vermont to Joseph Sr. and Lucy Mack on December 23, 1805. Both of his parents were dissenters from the Puritanism of Jonathan Edwards and those who followed him. They stayed more or less aloof from established religions, preferring a mystically oriented personal faith. This was not at all uncommon on the American frontier in the late eighteenth and early nineteenth centuries. Lucy came to the marriage with a thousand-dollar dowry from her successful brother. This was enough to give the family a good start in building a prosperous farm in the Green Mountains of Vermont. Unfortunately, the prosperity did not continue. Joseph Sr. lost what little fortune they had when he invested in a moneymaking scheme, shipping wild ginseng from the Americas to China. The shipping agent absconded with the money. Penniless, the Smiths moved from place to place in Vermont. In 1816 they moved to a more prosperous farming community in Palmyra, New York.

Western New York, like most of America west of the Appalachians, was the scene of religious revivals at this time. There were very few educated ministers. In the religious chaos of the frontier, enthusiasts of every sort abounded. The years of Joseph's youth saw much religious division. There were Reformed Baptists, Hard Shell Baptists, Free Will Baptists, Seventh Day Baptists and many other sects within just this one denomination. The Methodists split four times between 1814 and 1830. The Shaker sect came to the Palmyra area in 1826. This group was known for whirling and "shaking" in paroxysms of religious fervor, and for "the gift of tongues." Another possible influence on Joseph was the colony of religious enthusiasts twenty-five miles from Palmyra who followed the "Universal Friend," Jemima Wilkinson. She claimed to be the Messiah. The followers who came to her colony were governed by her personal revelations and were assured that she was immortal. In short, Western New York in the 1820s was the scene, not of established churches, but of faith healers, circuit preachers, revivalists and many religious charlatans. Many were more attracted to personality rather than tradition.

Living in rural Vermont, New Hampshire and New York, and the son of poor farmers, Joseph had little if any formal education. He knew no financial stability, as his father reeled from one financial disaster to another. Those who knew him remembered that from his youth he always had a vivid imagination. They are unanimous in describing him as a great storyteller. Even as a child he was fascinated with the Indian mounds which were common in upstate New York. There were eight of these within a twelve-mile radius of the Smith home in Palmyra. All accounts have Joseph as a friendly youth who loved to entertain people with fanciful stories of early American Indian cultures. According to his mother Lucy, "He would describe the ancient inhabitants of this continent, their dress, mode of travelling, and the animals upon which they rode; their cities, their buildings, with every particular; their mode of warfare; and also their religious worship. This he would do with as much ease, seemingly, as if he had spent his whole life with them."[4]

The followers and the enemies of Joseph create dramatically different pictures of him as a youth in Palmyra. We can gather, both from Smith's autobiography and from interviews of his neighbors, that he never held down a regular job. From his earliest adulthood, he preferred to make a living by such dubious practices as treasure hunting and using "magic stones" to find water and (buried) precious objects. Such superstitions were not uncommon on the frontier, but Joseph seems to have been particularly drawn to magic as a means of financial gain. Martin Harris, one of the witnesses of the Book of Mormon, tells us that Joseph found his "seer stone" in a well and that he used it to find hidden objects. His method was to put the stone in a hat, close the hat tight around his face, and behold the location of a lost object or treasure that would appear to him. Apparently, Joseph did not see his career as a charlatan as a major moral issue. In his own words, "As is common to most, or all youths, I fell into many vices and follies. I have not, neither can it be sustained, in truth, been guilty of wrongdoing or injuring any man or society of men; and those imperfections to which I allude and for which I have often had occasion to lament, were of a light, and, too often, vain mind, exhibiting a foolish and trifling conversation."[5]

This claim by Joseph that he got into no uncommon troubles is belied by the court record of a trial of Joseph Smith in Bainbridge, New York in March 1826 (when Joseph was twenty-one years old). He was accused of being "a disorderly person and an imposter." In the transcript of the trial, Smith admitted involvement in magic arts and treasure hunting. He was found guilty of disturbing the peace. During the 1830s a number of locals from Palmyra were interviewed. Many reported his use of seer stones, incantations, and nighttime treasure hunts. Even if we take into account the understandable bias of the reporters, given Joseph's own admission in court, a picture of him as a young adult emerges. Smith reached adulthood making a living chiefly as a charlatan and scam artist. Critics' interpretation of the subsequent life of Joseph Smith is that he realized at some point that there was more money available from a pseudo-Christian scam than from a career as the 19th-century equivalent of a mentalist.

When did Joseph Smith's career as a prophet and seer really begin? In later years, he claimed to have had a vision at the age of fourteen. According to Joseph, he went into the woods, bewildered about the competing claims of the religious revivals around him, to inquire of the Lord directly.

> I kneeled down and began to offer up the desires of my heart to God. I had scarcely done so, when immediately I was seized upon by some power which entirely overcame me as to bind my tongue so that I could not speak... I saw a pillar of light exactly over my head, above the brightness of the sun which descended gradually until it fell upon me... I saw two personages, whose brightness and glory defy all description, standing above me in the air. One of them spoke unto me, calling me by name, and said—pointing to the other—"This is my beloved Son, hear him."

According to his account, Joseph had sufficient presence of mind to ask a question that would be vital to his future religious career.

> ...I asked the Personages who stood above me in the light, which of the sects was right—and which I should join. I was answered that I must join none of them, for they were all wrong, and the Personage who addressed me said that all their creeds were an abomination in His sight... He again forbade me to join with any of them: and many other things did he say unto me, which I cannot write at this time.[6]

A question comes to mind at this point. Did Joseph actually have some sort of religious experience when he was fourteen years old, or is this a complete fabrication? A Christian will easily dismiss his interpretation that Joseph literally saw the Father and the Son in this vision, but perhaps it is possible he had some sort of dream which morphed into the final version. The problem is that his story of the event changed so often. In *History of the Church* (1840), Joseph claimed that his vision "excited a great deal of prejudice against me" at the time it was received. Yet there is no record in Palmyra newspapers of his vision at the time, or at any time before he produced the *Book of Mormon*. In an earlier autobiography by Smith in 1834 there is no mention at all of a vision at age fourteen. There are two versions of this vision in the published accounts by Orson Pratt, *Remarkable Visions*. The version of the story Pratt published in 1831 has a vision in Smith's sixteenth rather than his fourteenth year, in which Joseph states "...the Lord opened the heavens upon me and I saw the Lord." There is no mention of two "Personages." Pratt's 1835 account of the vision has "two Personages" and "many angels." The final published version by Smith in 1840 changes the "two Personages" into the Father and his Son Jesus Christ, though with no angels. Oliver Cowdery published the first authorized Mormon history in 1834. There is no mention at all of a vision of the Father and the Son. Cowdery places the beginning of Smith's career as a visionary at the age of 18, in 1823. For Cowdery, Joseph's first vision was of the angel Moroni, when he told Joseph where to find the golden plates on which the Book of Mormon were recorded.

Some allowance can be made for one's memories to change over time, but this amount of change raises suspicions about whether Joseph Smith concocted the entire affair. In light of this supposed vision, it is worth noting that according to the records of the Presbyterian Church in Palmyra, the Smith family continued to attend until at least 1828. There is also a record of Joseph's attempt to join the local Methodist church on June 15, 1828. He was turned down because of his reputation as a seer and treasure hunter. Apparently, Joseph did not heed the command of "the Father and his Son Jesus Christ" to take part in no established religion.

By the age of nineteen, Joseph's reputation as a money digger and seer had spread sufficiently that Josiah Stowel came to see him all the way from Pennsylvania, "on account of having heard that he possessed certain keys by which he could discern things invisible to the natural eye."[7] Josiah's son, Simpson, talked Joseph into pursuing a treasure hunt for a lost Spanish silver mine in the Susquehanna Valley for wages of fourteen dollars a month, plus room and board. It was while engaged in searching for treasure for Stowell that Joseph boarded with Isaac Hale and found a different sort of treasure: He met his future wife, Emma Hale. She soon fell in love with the tall (six-foot), powerful, handsome Joseph Smith.

It was also during his work for Josiah Stowell that Joseph had his first serious brush with the law. A complaint was lodged against him by a neighbor of Josiah's, Peter Bridgman. Joseph was arrested for "being a disorderly person and an imposter."

Transcripts of the trial have been discovered. In his testimony, Joseph admitted that he had used a certain stone to determine where hidden treasures in the bowels of the earth were and that he had used the same stone to look for coined money and other lost property in Palmyra. Smith was found guilty of the charges.

Perhaps it was this trial, or perhaps it was repeated failure to find any treasures at all through use of his seeing stone, that convinced Joseph to move on to more fruitful endeavors. At the age of twenty-two he put behind himself his career as a treasure hunter (with one notable exception in 1835, as we will see later). He and twenty-four-year old Emma were in love. When he asked Isaac Hale for her hand in marriage, Emma's father refused his request, accusing Joseph of being a cheap imposter. Instead, Joseph married Emma in secret on January 18, 1827. It was only after a delay of eight months that Joseph braved a visit to Isaac Hale. He hired his friend Peter Ingersoll and his cart to make the trip. We have Ingersoll's version of the encounter.[8] Isaac's response? "You have stolen my daughter and married her. I had much rather have followed her to the grave." Upon seeing his new son-in-law, Isaac said, in tears, "You spend your time in digging for money—pretend to see in a stone, and thus try to deceive people." According to Peter Ingersoll, Joseph wept in turn and confessed that he could no longer see with the stone—that his former claims were all false. He promised to give up the nefarious profession. Perhaps he meant well, but we will see that this promise to his wife's father was not kept.

# Chapter 2

# Joseph Smith Begins a Movement

Eighteen months after his conviction on charges of disorderly conduct, Joseph Smith claims to have come into possession of the golden plates on which the Book of Mormon was written "in Reformed Egyptian script," and thus a new and more prosperous career for the handsome and charming young man began.

According to his own account, Smith first learned about the golden plates on which the words of Nephi were recorded on September 21, 1823. On this night, a figure "glorious beyond description, and his countenance truly like lightning" appeared to the young prophet. Calling Joseph by name, he identified himself as the angel Moroni. According to Joseph, "He said that there was a book deposited, written upon gold plates, giving an account of the former inhabitants of this continent, and the sources from which they sprang."[9] Smith claims that Moroni also told him that two stones, fastened to a breastplate and called the Urim and the Thummim, were deposited with the plates to assist in translating the tablets.

Joseph recorded that he went to the Hill Cumorah and saw the plates inside a stone box, but an angel told him that he was not yet pure enough to touch them. He visited the plates every year on the anniversary of his original discovery. Joseph claims to have waited four years to be given permission to view these precious documents. Yet it was during this time that he was most active in his money digging and was convicted of disturbing the peace. If we are to believe the account of both Joseph and his mother, Lucy, he finally dug up the golden plates on the Hill Cumorah in September 1827. Joseph said that he found them in a stone box, along with the Urim and Thummim and a sword he called the sword of Laban. Of course, Lucy was never allowed to see these plates, having been told that it would mean instant death, so her testimony is not strong on this account.

The *Book of Mormon* (1830) is a story of the origin of Native Americans, who it is claimed were Jewish immigrants to the New World. What is the source of this fantastic story? It is safe to reasonably conclude that it did not come by direct translation of golden plates in Reformed Egyptian, left as a record for a future prophet on the Hill Cumorah, in upstate New York.

Scholarly archaeology had its beginnings with the work of the French and the British in Egypt in the late eighteenth century. In the 1820s evidence-based archaeology and anthropology had not even begun in the Americas. A common theory, even among the educated at that time, was that the Native Americans were descended from the ten "lost" tribes of Israel. Never mind the fact that there really are no "lost" tribes of Israel—the northern tribes were "lost" through intermarriage and assimilation to pagan religion in surrounding nations (2 Kings 17). Unfortunately for the credibility of Joseph Smith, his story of the origin of the inhabitants of the Western Hemisphere cannot be sustained. Joseph's story of the Nephites, the Jaredites and the Lamanites, and his claim of the Jewish origins of the native tribes and the burial mounds around Palmyra, has been disproved. Linguistic, genetic and physical evidence all link the native people of the Americas with Eastern Asia.

Joseph Smith was not alone in espousing the theory that the indigenous people in North and South America derive from the ten lost tribes of Israel. The most influential preachers in British North America, including Roger Williams, William Penn, Cotton Mather and Jonathan Edwards[10] had all spoken of the natives as degenerate Israelites. The difference, of course, is that these men did not claim that their theories were an inspired second testament of Jesus Christ. It has been proposed that the most influential source for Joseph's imaginative story was the work of Ethan Smith, who published a book in 1823 titled *View of the Hebrews; or the Ten Tribes of Israel in America*. This was the same year that Joseph later claimed to have had his vision of the angel Moroni, seven years before his Book of Mormon. Ethan Smith's theory was that the Indians were degenerate remnants of the Ten Lost Tribes of Israel, who had destroyed the less civilized peoples they found in the Americas, but who later fell into an uncivilized state, waiting for the coming of the white race to the Americas. This is the essence of the Book of Mormon. Given that the basic plot line of the Book of Mormon was available to Smith at the time he wrote it, we have good reason to be skeptical that he received the Book of Mormon from buried golden plates, deposited over one thousand three hundred years before they were discovered and translated by Smith.

Other sources for the Book of Mormon have been proposed. Many books supporting the Ten Tribe theory of Native American origins were in print when Joseph published his book. For example, there is Josiah Priest's *The Wonders of Nature and the Providence Displayed*, published in 1825, which adds some stories about the plague of darkness that are included nearly word for word in the Book of Mormon.

The secretaries Joseph employed for writing down the "translation" of the golden plates varied. At first it was his wife, Emma, who did the recording. She never saw the plates, although they were often left near her, wrapped in a linen cloth. Later, she claimed to have actually picked up the linen-wrapped plates, reporting that "They seemed to be pliable, like thick paper, and would rustle with a metallic sound when the edges were moved by the thumb as one does sometimes thumb the edges of a book."[11] As we will see, Joseph had used a "prophecy" to fill his wife with dread about the danger to her life if she looked at the actual plates. Surely she must have been tempted to unwrap the linen and glance at the plates, but according to her own words, she never did.

The story Joseph and Emma Smith, Oliver Cowdery, David Whitmer, and Martin Harris told of the actual "translation" of the golden plates is a fascinating one. According to his own testimony, David Whitmer was an eyewitness to the actual process of translation. He said "Joseph Smith would put the seer stone into a hat, and put his face in the hat, drawing it closely around his face to exclude the light; and in the darkness the spiritual light would shine. A piece of something representing parchment would appear, and on that appeared the writing. One character at a time would appear and, under it was the interpretation in English. Brother Joseph would read off the English to Oliver Cowdery, his principal scribe, and when it was written down and repeated to Brother Joseph to see if it was correct, then it would disappear, and another character with the interpretation would appear."[12]

The work of translating proceeded relatively slowly with Emma, so Joseph turned to Martin Harris. He worked in a room divided by a blanket over a rope, with Joseph using the Urim and the Thummim on one side, and Martin recording the results of the translation on the other. By this time, the "plates" were kept in a small wooden chest. Martin was a major financial backer of the project. Perhaps motivated by the skeptical criticism of his wife, Martin demanded to see the plates. Joseph refused. Given that Harris was the major source of funding for his project, Joseph had no choice but to give him something to go on. Finally, he agreed to give Harris a page on which he claimed he had transcribed a copy of what was on one of the plates. He informed Harris that the plates were not written in Hebrew, but in "Reformed Egyptian." Harris took this manuscript for confirmation of its truly ancient origins to Samuel L. Mitchell, vice president of Rutgers Medical College. Mitchell was not an enthusiast of the theory of the Jewish origin of the Native Americans. Nevertheless, he referred Harris to a colleague who was more of an expert in ancient languages, Charles Anthon. Anthon was a professor of Greek and Latin at Columbia College (now Columbia University).

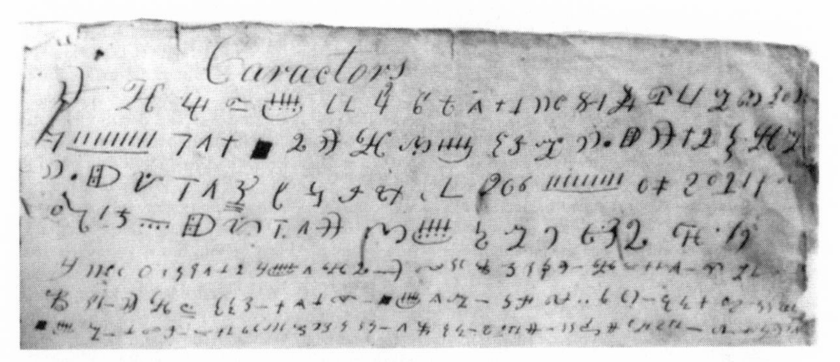


*Characters from the "Anthon Manuscript" said to have been copied from the Golden Plates by Joseph Smith and given to Oliver Cowdery*

Perhaps Smith was thinking that he would be able to pull off his fraud, at least for the foreseeable future, banking on the hope that his ruse of "Reformed Egyptian" would remain secret for many years. Joseph may not have been aware that the Egyptian hieroglyphs on the Rosetta Stone had already been translated by Jean-Francois Champollion in 1822. Unfortunately for believers in the work of Joseph Smith, Anthon did not confirm that the golden plates were legitimate. On the contrary, he reported that what he was shown by Martin Harris "consisted of all kinds of crooked characters disposed in columns, and had evidently been prepared by some person who had before him at the time a book containing various alphabets. Greek and Hebrew letters, crosses and flourishes, Roman letters inverted or placed sideways, were arranged in perpendicular columns, and the whole ended in a rude delineation of a circle divided into various compartments, decked with various strange marks and evidently copied after the Mexican calendar by Humboldt, but copied in a way as not to betray the source whence it was derived." He declared that Smith's claim to be working from "Reformed Egyptian" to be "totally false."[13] We can see from the description of Anthon that, although this was clearly a fraud, it was a clever one, sufficient to fool someone as credulous as Martin Harris.

After completing 116 pages of the manuscript of the Book of Mormon, in June 1828, Harris begged for time off and for an opportunity to show the work to his ever-skeptical wife. During the time off, Emma gave birth; the child died at birth. Unfortunately for Joseph, Martin's wife, Lucy, stole the manuscript from her husband, taunting

Martin that, "If this be a divine communication, the same being who revealed it to you can easily replace it."[14] We can appreciate the healthy skepticism of Lucy and imagine her frustration with a husband so easily duped by Joseph Smith.

What was Smith to do? If he were to "re-translate" what had already been written, his fraud would be revealed, at least to Martin Harris. If Lucy were to later produce the original manuscript, the fraud would be made obvious to the whole world. After what must have been a period of great doubt, he decided to bring forth what can only be seen as a very convenient new revelation from God. To meet the need to cover the same time period in the history of the Native Americans, God provided Joseph with an alternative version on the "plates of Nephi." Joseph says that he was forbidden to re-translate the first 116 pages. Where and when these new plates were found by Joseph is never revealed. God told Joseph that he was to start with the plates of Nephi; only after this translation of these plates was completed was he to take up with the original golden plates, beginning from page 117 of the manuscript.

From this time forward, it appears that Joseph Smith's vision for the Book of Mormon and his future as a religious leader sharpened. The work proceeded at a much faster pace. At some time in the winter of 1828/29 Joseph and Martin took up the work again. In April, Harris was replaced by the reliable and somewhat more educated Oliver Cowdery, who, at twenty-two years of age, was only one year younger than Joseph. Just three months later, the original manuscript of the Book of Mormon, at 275,000 words, was ready to be printed.

We will reserve a detailed discussion of the content of this book, and the changes it underwent in the earliest editions, to a future chapter. Let us now settle for an extremely short summary. The book published by Joseph Smith in July 1829 is the story of two separate bands of Jewish refugees traveling across the Atlantic and landing somewhere in Central America. Although the Book of Mormon does not actually specify Central America, when one reads the book, it is the only geographical location that seems to fit. Mormons agree with this location for the scenes in the book. The first group, the Jaredites, left Mesopotamia after the fall of the Tower of Babel. They followed their leader, Jared, in eight watertight vessels across the sea, landing in the New World some time before 2000 BC. They established populations in the New World, fought many battles amongst themselves, being finally wiped out in a battle with the Lamanites, who were the predecessors of the modern Native Americans.

A second wave of Jews came to the Americas in "the first year of King Zedekiah" (about 600 BC). Fleeing persecution in Judah, The Nephites, followers of Nephi, came to the same area of Central America where the Jaredites had landed. They fought one fantastic battle after another against the Lamanites. The Nephites were more righteous and whiter, while the Lamanites were generally less godly, and therefore had darker skin. The Nephites preached the gospel of Jesus Christ (hundreds of years before he was born!) and followed the Old Testament laws as well. Jesus came and preached to these Nephites in his resurrected body after his work in Palestine was done. War upon war continued, and many Lamanites were converted. They became more light-skinned as a result. Finally, continued warfare resulted in the complete destruction of the Nephites and the temporary end of Christianity in the New World. The final Nephite, Moroni, wrote down the Book of Mormon on the golden plates and buried them (in upstate New York?) for later discovery by God's chosen one.

Two challenges to the final publication of the Book of Mormon remained. First, Joseph Smith had promised that God would choose three eyewitnesses to the actual golden plates. For this honor he chose Martin Harris, Oliver Cowdery, and David Whitmer. In a now-famous scene, in Smith's version of the event, he said to the three, "Behold, I say unto you, that you must rely upon my word, which if you do with full purpose of heart, you shall have a view of the plates and also the breastplate, the sword of Laban, the Urim and the Thummim... And it is by your faith that you shall obtain a view of them."[15] According to Smith, the four men walked into the woods and knelt in prayer, waiting for a miracle. After a time of tense quiet, Harris, full of doubt and blaming the lack of miracle on his own doubt, asked to be allowed to pray by himself. After a time of further prayer, according to Smith,

> We knelt down in prayer, when presently we beheld a light above us in the air, of exceeding brightness; and behold, an angel stood before us. In his hands he held the plates which we had been praying for these to have a view of. He turned over the leaves one by one, so that we could see them, and discern the engravings thereon distinctly. He then addressed himself to David Whitmer, and said, 'David, blessed is the Lord, and he that keeps his commandments;' when, immediately afterwards, we heard a voice from out of the bright light above us, saying, 'These plates have been revealed by the power of God, and they have been translated by the power of God. The translation of them which you have seen is correct, and I command you to bear record of what you now see and hear."

Immediately after this, Joseph found Harris. They prayed together further. Finally, the same vision came to Martin as had been experienced by the others. He sprang to his feet, shouting, "Tis enough; tis enough; mine eyes have beheld; mine eyes have beheld; Hosanna, Hosanna, blessed be the Lord."[16]

The testimony of these three witnesses is found on the front page of every copy of the Book of Mormon, declaring that they saw a vision of "the golden plates and the engravings thereon." Our confidence in this essential Mormon claim is somewhat reduced by Harris' later testimony to a resident of Palmyra that, "I did not see them as I do that pencil-case, yet I saw them with the eye of faith; I saw them just as distinctly as I see anything around me—though they were covered with a cloth."[17]

The press in the Palmyra area at the time published similar but not identical accounts of their vision from the three witnesses. This is evidence that Smith was able somehow to convince them that they truly had some sort of "vision" in the woods. Perhaps he had an ability to mesmerize his followers, or maybe he induced them to consider the possible financial benefit to seeing such a vision. We cannot know for sure. The reliability of these principal witnesses to the Book of Mormon is deficient. Cowdery later left Mormonism to become a Methodist, declaring publicly that he was ashamed for having been associated with Mormonism. No less than Joseph Smith himself described Martin Harris twice in *Doctrine and Covenants* as "a wicked man."[18] Harris later converted to Quakerism, and still later back to Mormonism. David Whitmer also left the Mormon movement.

The Book of Mormon also lists eight witnesses to the golden plates in addition to the three. Three of these eight witnesses were members of Smith's family, four were from the Whitmer clan, and the eighth witness, Hiram Page, was married to a Whitmer daughter. Three of the eight later disavowed their allegiance to Joseph Smith. The other five all died before Joseph did. The matter of proving the reality of the golden plates was conveniently settled when Joseph Smith announced that the angel Moroni had taken the golden plates back to heaven.

Financing the publication of the Book of Mormon was the second challenge for Joseph. Martin Harris agreed to mortgage his farm to finance the first edition. However, a group of citizens of Palmyra organized a boycott, and the financier demanded cash. Joseph had a "revelation" instructing Cowdery and Hiram Page to go to Toronto, where they would find a man anxious to buy the copyright. When this revelation failed to materialize, Smith had a second revelation directed to Martin Harris, "And again, I command thee that thou shall not covet thine own property, but impart it freely to the printing of the Book of Mormon."[19] The revelation included a threat that Harris would see the destruction of himself and his property. By this time, Martin's wife had left him. Martin was free to act. Harris duly sold his farm, and the Book of Mormon was published on March 26, 1830.

The publication of the Book of Mormon was a significant event in Western New York. The followers of the erstwhile prophet swelled to forty within a month. His followers went on tour promoting and selling copies of the Golden Book. What may have been a scheme to profit from a book about the origins of the American Indians was quickly transformed into the means of launching a new religion. One month after the Book of Mormon was published, Joseph publicly declared himself to be, "a Seer, a Translator, a Prophet, an Apostle of Jesus Christ and Elder of the Church through the will of God the Father and the grace of your Lord Jesus Christ." This is the role Joseph stepped into and assumed until his death thirteen years later. Within two years of the publishing of the Book of Mormon, Joseph was claiming that the movement he established was the true, restored Church of Jesus Christ.

All did not go smoothly, however, for Joseph. There were two attempts to have him arrested for disorderly conduct. One succeeded, but he was acquitted. A mob tried to tar and feather him, but he escaped with the help of a constable. His wife hesitated to commit to his movement. She refused baptism for six weeks and resisted "confirmation" still longer. It required a revelation on the part of Joseph to convince her to rely on converts to the movement for their financial support, and finally, one month later, she submitted to the ceremony.

Another early challenge to his movement came from within the inner circle. If Joseph could have personal visions, why could his closest associates not have similar revelations? Oliver Cowdery began to write his own revelations, and even to challenge some of Joseph's teachings. Hiram Page began to use a "seer stone"[20] of his own, with two holes drilled through it. Was this going to be a general charismatic movement, with competing modern-day prophets, and all the potential for anarchy such a movement threatened? Joseph received a revelation dealing with this problem: "No one shall be appointed to receive commandments and revelations in this Church, except Joseph Smith."[21] Problem solved. This was a smart move by Joseph Smith. It allowed him to prevent the disintegration of his new religion.

It is time to step back from the story. What are we to make of Joseph Smith? A number of possibilities come to mind. One is that he was a charlatan and a convincing liar, intent on taking his religious scam to its logical conclusion, exploiting others for personal fame, fortune and power. Another line of thinking is that he was delusional; that he had psychologically induced dreams which he transformed into "visions"[22] and that he really believed he had spoken with God and Jesus Christ. Smith thought himself to be the true prophet of God, with the salvation of the whole world in his hands. The first option seems more reasonable, yet it raises some questions. Did Smith not realize that his scheme would culminate in his early demise? As his megalomaniacal self-proclamation spun out of control, surely he must have realized at some point that the only possible end for him was ridicule, persecution and possibly death. Would anyone in full possession of his faculties have maintained the scam, even in the face of death?

Perhaps for an extremely confident person like Joseph Smith the answer was yes—it was worth the price.

A third view is a combination of the first two scenarios. Perhaps as his religious fraud unfolded, Joseph began to believe in the image he had created of himself—not that he had seen God or translated golden plates in Reformed Egyptian, but that he was invincible. He began to believe he was the greatest man of his time, a true religious genius, with fate on his side. Such a legacy was worth the persecution or chance of death, especially if sweetened with a very fulfilling life while it lasted. If this picture of Joseph Smith is close to the truth, then there is irony, borne out by history. The approximately fifteen million followers of the prophet from Palmyra today are testimony to this picture. The conclusion of Fawn Brodie is appropriate: "At an early period he seems to have reached an inner equilibrium that permitted him to pursue his career with a highly compensated but nevertheless very real sincerity. Certainly a persisting consciousness of guilt over the cunning and deception with which his prophetic career was launched would eventually have destroyed him." [23] On a day-to-day basis, Smith appears to have put himself into the minds of his believers and, in a way hard to comprehend, to have come to believe his own rhetoric.

A fourth view—the one put forth by the modern LDS—cannot be sustained by the evidence. This is the view that Joseph Smith was the prophet of God and God's chosen instrument to restore the gospel hidden for more than 1700 years before he was chosen to lead God's children back to the Latter-day Zion.

# Chapter 3

# From Palmyra to Kirtland, to Far West, Missouri

## Palmyra to Kirtland

The story of Joseph Smith and the movement he founded in 1830 now gains momentum. We will see a number of major episodes unfold, and it will be hard to believe the entire tale occupied only the fourteen years which ended in the violent death of the self-proclaimed prophet at a jail in Carthage, Illinois, in June of 1844.

It soon became painfully clear to Smith that the proverb "a prophet is without honor only in his home town and in his own house" (Matthew 13:57) applied to him. The locals were too well aware of his earlier misdeeds—ones which paralleled his new, prophetic claims—for him to ever be able to establish peacefully a basis for his ministry at Palmyra. To this end, Joseph published a revelation that the New Zion was to be built "on the borders, by the Lamanites."[24]

This implied two things to the early followers of Joseph Smith. It meant movement of the church to the West, and it implied that attempts needed to be made to convert the "red man." In the book of Mormon, it had been prophesied concerning the Native Americans, "..and many generations shall not pass away among them, save they shall be a white and delightsome people" (2 Nephi 30:6). This racist idea was not original to Joseph Smith, but his use of it is offensive to our sensibilities today.

Joseph sent Oliver Cowdery on a mission to convert the Indians and to look for a place to build the New Jerusalem. It is at this point that the very young Mormon movement came into contact with the Restoration movement of Alexander Campbell. Thomas Campbell and his son Alexander and those associated with them had started a movement in the 1820s that for a number of years was to run parallel to the Mormon movement. This was a primitivist church movement attempting to "restore" Christianity to its pristine unity, based on the Bible alone, without the denominational infighting which dominated the religious scene in the United States at the time. The Campbellites were in one sense the exact opposite of the Mormons. Theirs was an intellectual/rational Christianity, closely tied to the Bible, denying any sort of modern-day revelation or emotional work of the Holy Spirit. Yet while in one sense the two movements were opposites, in another they were twins. Both offered a vision of a primitive sort of Christianity destined to rise above the petty partisan spirit of the denominations. In one significant aspect, the vision offered by Joseph Smith was the same as that of Alexander Campbell. Both offered a kind of utopian picture of a universal Church, composed of "saints" with a common vision and purpose.

On Cowdery's expedition to the West, he met a recent convert to Campbell's movement who had subsequently been pulled into the orbit of Joseph Smith. His name was Parley Pratt. He had been converted to the Restorationist Campbellite movement in Ohio, but under the spell of Hyrum Smith, joined with the Mormons. Parley and his brother Orson eventually played a major role in the Mormon Church, both as evangelists and as intellectual leaders of the movement. To Ohio the Cowdery mission went.

There they came into contact with another Campbellite by the name of Sidney Rigdon. Rigdon was to have more influence on the thinking and theology of Joseph Smith than perhaps anyone else. He became Smith's right hand man and in many ways his alter ego. Rigdon was one of the most successful preachers in the Campbell movement, bringing thousands into what became the Stone-Campbell churches.

Rigdon was of a mercurial temperament. In modern terms, he would probably be diagnosed with severe depression. He was often visited by "nervous spasms and swooning." The polar opposite of his mentor, Alexander Campbell, he was strongly inclined to believe in the miraculous intervention of the Holy Spirit, and to see his spasms and swoonings as the result of the work of the Holy Spirit. Alexander Campbell, on the other hand, was an empiricist who was suspicious of any modern-day manifestation of the Holy Spirit. Rigdon was strongly attracted to millennialist thinking. He had established a communistic colony of disciples in Kirtland Ohio, close to Cleveland. It was over his communistic thinking and his interest in modern-day prophecy and speaking in tongues that Rigdon broke with Campbell. Eventually, he brought many into the fledgling Latter-day Saints. Nearly the entire commune in Kirtland was baptized into the Mormon Church. This was the first big victory for Joseph's young religious movement.

A side comment deserves mention at this point. It is hard to miss the parallels between Joseph Smith and Islam's prophet, Muhammad. Both claimed an angelic visitor announcing that they were God's final prophet. Both had relatively little success in their hometowns, and were persecuted, and at times faced the real possibility of death. Muhammad fled from Mecca to Medina, where he converted many and his movement gathered momentum. Smith fled from Palmyra to Kirtland, Ohio, where he converted many and Mormonism experienced a boom. Other parallels between the two "prophets" can be seen. We know from his writings and speeches that Joseph recognized and played on the parallels between himself and Muhammad.[26]

Let's now return to our story. Rigdon's break with Alexander Campbell had a deep effect on his former mentor. Within a few months, Alexander wrote the first clearly thought-out refutation of the teachings of Joseph Smith and of his Book of Mormon, published in Campbell's *Millennial Harbinger* (Volume II, February, 1831). In 1832 it was published in booklet form as *Delusions: An Analysis of the Book of Mormon*. The *Millennial Harbinger* document is printed in the Appendix and is well worth the time to read, as it is one of the most well-argued refutations of the Book of Mormon.[27]

In the meantime, Joseph had conceived of a bold plan to reveal a new inspired book to his followers, both to seal his authority and to solve a few current practical and theological problems. He had already toyed with the idea of revealing a lost book. Joseph was sufficiently confident of the credulity of his followers to dictate to Oliver Cowdery a fragment he claimed had been buried by the apostle John. This was originally published as a small section on his *Book of Commandments*. Later, it was expanded upon and became Section 7 in the *Doctrine and Covenants*, which comprises part of the Mormon canon, along with the *Book of Mormon* and *The Pearl of Great Price*. He then revealed an alleged conversation between Moses and God, which had not been included in the Pentateuch. This document is known as *The Book of Moses*. He claimed also that he would eventually reveal what he called *The Book of Enoch*. *The Book of Moses* and *The Book of Abraham* were compiled and published as *The Pearl of Great Price*. We will provide a more thorough treatment of these writings in a later chapter.

Looking at Joseph's writings beginning in 1832 gives one the impression that his vision for what the Mormon religion was to become sharpened at this point. He expanded considerably the biblical claim about Enoch that "God took him away" (Genesis 5:24). In his revelation Joseph claimed that Enoch had founded a City of Holiness named Zion. This city, a model of a godly community, was taken directly to heaven. But, in the last days, when "truth I will send forth out of the earth [Moses 7:62, an obvious reference to the Golden Plates] then the heavenly Zion will be transported back to the earth...and it will be called Zion a New Jerusalem." The only remaining question was: Where will the new, Latter-day Zion be built? The search for the site of the New

Jerusalem occupied a great portion of the energy of the movement until Smith's death.

Sidney Rigdon caught on immediately to this vision, stepping in to become second only to Joseph in the movement. He suggested to Smith that they move to his Kirtland community to establish this Zion. In David Whitmer's words, Rigdon "soon worked himself deep into Brother Joseph's affections, and had more influence over him than any other man living. He was Brother Joseph's private counselor and his most intimate friend and brother for some time after they met."[28]

Joseph overcame steep opposition to convince his sixty followers to move all the way from Palmyra, New York, to Kirtland, Ohio. In January 1831, they set off to their new home with great hopes for the future, but many were wary of the growing influence of Sidney Rigdon over Smith. In Kirtland, Joseph joined a group of followers greater than his entire church in New York. However, he faced significant challenges to his authority. Many in Rigdon's sect felt they had the ability to have personal revelation. Joseph saw the danger in this, as revivalist movements with uncontrolled self-revelation typically splinter into competing groups. Wisely, Joseph made nearly every male member of his group a "priest," as long as each would completely submit to the leadership and authority of Elder Joseph Smith. There was to be no unauthorized personal revelation, upon pain of being driven from the church. Joseph applied biblical titles such as deacon, elder, bishop and, of course, apostle to create a hierarchy of increasingly dedicated church members. This had the effect of producing a church that had virtually no professional ministry. The fellowship of the believers was simple and informal, yet it had a strong hierarchy, with sufficient authority coming from the top to contain the enthusiasms of an emotional religious sect. Whether we like the Mormon Church or not, we will have to admit that this decision has contributed to the strength of the continuing Mormon movement. Joseph Smith was brilliant as an organizer of men.

Over the next five years thousands streamed to Kirtland, from New England, New York, Ohio and elsewhere. Smith developed into a powerful preacher who could keep crowds spellbound, alternating between laughter and tears, for hours on end. Following the pattern set by Sidney Rigdon, Smith established a communistic organization in Kirtland for his followers. Each member was to turn over all his or her worldly goods to the trust of the United Order of Enoch. This provided a strong incentive for members of the church not to apostatize, as Joseph decreed in a new revelation that "he that sinneth and repenteth not shall be cast out and shall not receive again that which he has consecrated unto me."[29] As we will see, the establishment of the all-encompassing communistic United Order turned out to be an ill-advised move for the church in the end.

## Zion Revealed: Independence, Missouri

In the meantime, Joseph's missionaries were out searching for the Lamanites and seeking a site to build his Zion—his New Jerusalem. Oliver Cowdery was convinced that Independence, Missouri was the ideal site for the heavenly city. Parley Pratt also brought back positive reports from Jackson County in Northern Missouri.

A general council was called in Kirtland. Joseph announced the reestablishment on earth of the Priesthood of Melchizedek. He began to announce the appointment of his key men as high priests. In a fit of enthusiasm, he sought to heal a number of those in attendance, but failed in his efforts. This resulted in closing the conference sooner than planned. Many were disillusioned. Joseph announced that miracles could not be performed in Ohio because it was not the land of Zion. Joseph dropped the shocking news that he was moving with thirty disciples to Missouri to establish the New Jerusalem.

Within months, in the Spring of 1831, his weary New York converts began to move to open land just west of Independence, Missouri, the location of modern Kansas City. Independence at that time was a tiny outpost, the last town and launching point for settlers traveling on the Santa Fe Trail to New Mexico. Here, they were on the very edge of white settlement, with Native Americans their neighbors. Soon after arriving, Joseph chose and dedicated the site for his future temple. Sidney Rigdon, among others, refused to stay at this bleak outpost on the edge of civilization. A small group of those dispossessed of land in Ohio stayed behind in Independence, and Joseph returned to Kirtland.

Joseph then began to work on his personal revision of the Bible. This was key to his work, as he had already declared that the Bibles used by the Catholic and Protestant churches were corrupted. This new endeavor was necessary to support his claim that all Christians had apostatized before the Church was reestablished by Joseph Smith. His revised Bible was not published during his lifetime, but the "translation" was published by the Reorganized Mormons in 1867.[30] This document gives us insight into how his theology developed. In Joseph Smith's Bible revision, a prophecy was inserted into Genesis. Smith has Joseph, son of Jacob say, "Thus saith the Lord God of my fathers unto me, 'A choice seer will I raise up out of the fruit of thy loins, and he shall be esteemed highly among the fruit of thy loins...and his name shall be called Joseph, and it shall be after the name of his father." In which Hebrew manuscript Joseph found this insertion was, of course, never explained. Neither was Joseph able to resist amplifying Isaiah 29. In Smith's version Isaiah makes reference to the Book of Mormon and the return of the golden plates to the Lord.

Perhaps more significant to the development of Mormon theology was Smith's discovery, along with Rigdon, of a new interpretation of 1 Corinthians 15:40. In this passage, Paul talks about the fact that there are earthly and heavenly bodies, each with a different degree of splendor. Smith and Rigdon found in this passage three kinds of bodies, three possible final states and three kingdoms in heaven after the resurrection. This led to the doctrine of celestial, terrestrial and telestial bodies, and a kind of universalism[31] in Mormonism not found in the Book of Mormon. This doctrine will be discussed in a later chapter.

While Joseph worked on his Bible revision in the town of Hiram, near Kirtland, an unpleasant episode occurred in March 1832. A drunken mob of Mormon-haters dragged both Smith and Rigdon from Joseph's house. They stripped Joseph naked, savagely beat him, and tarred and feathered him. Rigdon was also badly beaten by the mob. They threatened to castrate Smith, claiming he had shown too much interest in a young girl. Fortunately for Joseph, the doctor brought along to perform the surgery refused to do it. Joseph recovered sufficiently to drag his bleeding body back to his house, where Emma cleaned him up. To the astonishment of his attackers, Joseph preached the next day, as scheduled, and chose not even to mention the atrocious acts of his enemies. Naturally, his reputation as a hero was greatly enhanced by this event.

In order to quell a possible rebellion in Independence, Joseph paid a brief visit to Missouri in 1832 during which he united the finances of Kirtland and Independence into one communal United Order. Another significant event that year was the arrival in Kirtland of a sturdy Vermonter by the name of Brigham Young. Smith was immediately captured by Brigham's zeal, intelligence, obvious talent, and strong character. That evening, when Young began to speak in tongues, Joseph did not impose his usual reluctance to accept the miraculous gifts, but instead pronounced that Brigham had spoken the true language of Adam.

The year 1833 marked the beginning of Joseph's efforts to build a temple suitable to his ambition. Foundations were laid for temples both in Kirtland and in Zion (Independence, Missouri). By this time the group in Independence had swelled to 1200, and in Kirtland the number of followers was only slightly smaller. Other important events occurred in this seemingly auspicious year for Smith's church.

The year did not end as auspiciously as it had begun. In 1833 Smith published his now famous revelation known as the Word of Wisdom.[32] Here Joseph suggested that his followers abstain from alcohol, tea, coffee and tobacco in order to enter the celestial kingdom. This suggestion later became a commandment within the church. It was to remain controversial throughout the ministry of Joseph Smith as it was well known in his inner circle that Joseph was not averse to smoking a cigar and to drinking alcohol. A number of references to Joseph's drinking in the *History of the Church* have since been removed by the church hierarchy. (In fairness to Smith, there is no evidence that he had an addiction to coffee, tobacco, or alcohol).

Another significant event in 1833 was the publication in Independence of his *Book of Commandments*. This was a compilation of the many revelations of Joseph Smith. The press in Independence was destroyed by a mob before the first printing of the revelations was completed. The project was taken up again in 1835 in Kirtland. This time the collection was given the title *Doctrine and Covenants*. By this date, the main components of the official "scripture" of Mormonism were nearing completion (*Book of Mormon, Pearl of Great Price, Doctrine and Covenants*).

## Expulsion from Independence

Before Joseph's order to lay the cornerstone for the temple in Independence reached that city, a severe persecution broke out against his followers there. The violence which ensued cannot be justified, but it is not hard to see why they were not welcomed in Independence with open arms. Inspired by Joseph's own words, his followers publicly declared that "The Gentiles of this country are to be cut off, and their lands appropriated by us for inheritances."[33] It became clear to the locals that if the trend continued, soon the sheriff and the judges would all be either Mormon or in the pockets of the Mormons. Moreover, the Mormons strongly opposed slavery—in a state committed to the South and to slavery. Hundreds signed a declaration that they would pledge lives, fortunes and sacred honor to rid Independence of the Mormons, "after a timely warning."[34] Those signing this inflammatory pledge included the county clerk, the constable, the jailer and the judge of the court. The Mormon press was destroyed by a mob; many were dragged off, tarred and feathered. The mob demanded that the leaders of the church agree to abandon Independence and Jackson County or face a death sentence. The leaders agreed to this demand and the church was forced into exile. Houses were burned and storehouses were robbed by the Mormon haters. When the Saints asked for justice, they were rebuffed by every judge they faced.

To his credit, Joseph Smith produced a "revelation" on this occasion that the saints were to "renounce war, and proclaim peace, and to bear with all indignities with patience."[35] When attacks continued, even after the Mormons had agreed to leave, the settlers armed themselves. A small skirmish in which two marauders and one Mormon were killed was used as an excuse to threaten death to the Mormon prisoners and to disarm the Mormon militia. When this was completed, a mob, no longer fearful of reprisal, burned and looted nearly all the Mormon homes, violently driving the Latter-day Saints from their settlements. In the end, the Missouri press came to the support of the beleaguered Mormons, calling to account the outrageous behavior of the mob and of the civic leaders in Independence. However, the deed was done, and the Saints were through in Independence. With the destruction of their storehouses, the communistic United Order fell apart in both Independence and Kirtland. The brief attempt at communal living was subsequently abandoned.

His followers were mystified about why Joseph appeared to do nothing to defend his people in Zion. While they were being driven from their homes, he went on a preaching tour in Canada. Joseph decided that his inaction was sufficiently discouraging to his followers that something had to be done. He agreed to the organization of an army known as "Zion's Camp" at Kirtland, with the purpose of a march to Independence to relieve the persecuted members there. In May 1834 an army of more than 200 men set off on the 800-mile trek from Kirtland to Independence. This was no wagon train of new settlers. It was clearly a military expedition. The troops were led by Joseph Smith and spurred on by Sidney Rigdon, who announced that from now on followers of Joseph Smith were to be called the Church of Latter-day Saints, rather than simply the Church of Christ.

Along the way, Joseph trained the troops in military tactics. Their approach aroused the locals, who called out their own militia. Having lost the advantage of surprise, the Mormon army was outnumbered and outgunned. Their expected army of angels never appeared. When Zion's camp was hit with a cholera epidemic, the entire venture failed, and Joseph Smith retreated to Kirtland in shame. In response to his people's complaint about his autocratic rule, he changed his title to President of the High Priesthood.

An interesting aspect of Joseph Smith is his interest in education. It seems this interest was sincere, and it has infused his followers with a similar respect for education. This has had a positive effect on Mormons to the present day. From the beginning in Missouri, the Mormon settlers built schools. Joseph built up an academy in Kirtland (1834–35), which taught Greek, Hebrew, English grammar, geography, and other subjects.[36] Joseph himself pursued learning zealously. His tutors reported him an avid student, especially of foreign languages. However, he may have taken his confidence in his own learning too far. Smith once declared of himself, "I know more than all the world put together." He claimed to be able to translate seventeen different languages.[37] His overweening pride in this area contributed to one of Joseph's most embarrassing errors when he "translated" the *Book of Abraham*. Joseph's successor Brigham Young had virtually no interest in education, but fortunately for the movement, Smith's attention to education stayed with his followers.

In the summer of 1835 Joseph received a guest by the name of Michael Chandler. Chandler had been touring the West with four Egyptian mummies. He also had in his possession a number of ancient Egyptian papyrus scrolls, which experts in New York and Philadelphia had been unable to translate. He had heard of Smith's prowess as a translator of ancient documents, and so he came to Kirtland. Joseph—ever fascinated by anything ancient, especially things Egyptian—took the bait. Little did Smith know that Jean-Francois Champollion had recently translated the Rosetta Stone, making it now possible to assess the reliability of any interpretation of Egyptian hieroglyphs. The fact was not revealed publicly until 1837. Joseph pronounced that one of the papyri was written by the biblical Abraham and another by Joseph. What a coincidence that these documents, written by the biblical patriarchs themselves, found their way into Smith's hands in Kirtland!

Joseph had already decided to put away his translator stone, as well as the Urim and Thummim. Instead, he took another approach to translating these documents. He tried to create an Egyptian alphabet and grammar, on the basis of which he planned to translate the Egyptian texts. Finally, he gave up the project in frustration, only to be given an inspired translation by direct inspiration from heaven (according to Joseph Smith, anyway). This "translation" became the *Book of Abraham*, now found in *The Pearl of Great Price*. Smith never produced a translation of the papyrus he said was written by Joseph, son of Jacob.

The *Book of Abraham* was a watershed for Joseph Smith and Mormonism. Here we begin to see some of his decidedly un-Christian theology. It includes Smith's version of the creation story. Rather than "In the beginning, God created the heavens and the earth," Smith's "translation" has "The Gods organized the earth" (Abraham 3:25). Here we have two startling claims, from a biblical perspective. A little knowledge of the biblical languages can be a dangerous thing in the wrong hands. Smith's use of language illustrates this point. He had been exposed to the fact that the Hebrew word for God in Genesis chapter one is *Elohim*, which is plural. Smith put to paper in *The Book of Abraham* one of his most infamous innovations, the claim that there are many gods.

The second innovation contained in this little phrase in the *Book of Abraham* is the Mormon teaching that the universe is eternal. According to the writer of this little book, the gods of the earth simply rearranged pre-existing material to create the earth. Students of Joseph Smith's life[38] have speculated that Smith got this idea from a book he had recently read by Thomas Dick: *The Philosophy of a Future State*. In this essay, Dick supported the metaphysical idea that matter is eternal. We will have more to say about the theology of the *Book of Abraham* in a later chapter.

This document included Smith's theory of race. He claimed (or he had Abraham claim) that the Egyptians inherited the curse of black skin and an inferior status as a result of the curse of Ham. This was the standard argument of those who tried to use the Bible to support the institution of slavery. In 1835, Smith turned decisively against abolitionism to support slavery. He may have been motivated in part by concerns over the place of his movement in the slave-holding state of Missouri.

Joseph had created plausible deniability when he conveniently had the golden plates taken away to heaven. This was not the case with the papyri purported to contain the *Book of Abraham*. They were proudly displayed along with the mummies in Kirtland and Nauvoo, Illinois for a number of years. They were sold by a relative of Joseph after his death. Most reasonable people would probably conclude that Smith did not really "translate" the *Book of Abraham* from the Egyptian papyrus, even without the actual documents in hand. However for one hundred years it was not possible to prove the fraud. It was thought that the original had been destroyed in the Great Chicago Fire. This changed in 1967 when the original papyri were discovered in a storeroom in the Metropolitan Museum of Art in New York City. The markings found on the document confirmed that they were in fact the originals which had been in the possession of Joseph Smith. Unfortunately for the church and the reputation of Joseph Smith, scholars are unanimous that this papyrus has absolutely nothing to do with Abraham or the Old Testament story. In fact, it is a common Egyptian funerary text, similar to thousands which have been unearthed in Egypt.

Because of Smith's willingness to compromise with his enemies, the Latter-day Saints entered a period of two years of relative peace. During this time, Joseph was able to see the completion of his first temple in Kirtland. This was an impressive building, especially considering that it was located on the frontier. It was to set the pattern for the Mormons to build elaborate, impressive temples. There were two large auditoriums, with twelve seats for the twelve apostles at either end. The dedication ceremony on March 27, 1836, was an all-male affair, with elaborate and impressive rituals—another hallmark of Joseph Smith's religious genius. It was at this point that Joseph included foot washing and anointing as part of the temple ceremonies. The opening ceremony engendered much enthusiasm. Many of the leading men gave fantastic prophecies of the future, and many spoke in tongues, perhaps inspired in part by the wine which was drunk after a twenty-four hour fast. Smith and Cowdery prayed together behind a veil, claimed to the ecstatic crowd that they had seen "the Lord," and that Moses had spoken to them face-to-face, committing to them the keys of Israel and the ten tribes.

## Trouble in Kirtland, Ohio; Peace in Far West

It was at about this time that one of the darker sides of the character of Joseph Smith began to emerge. Rumors of his infidelity had spread previously, but evidence was lacking. In 1835 Emma took a seventeen year old orphan by the name of Fannie Alger into the Smith home. Rumors spread that Joseph was in love with the beautiful young girl. When she became pregnant a furious Emma drove Fannie out of the Smith home. According to Joseph Smith's grammar teacher at the time, "Emma was furious, and drove the girl, who was unable to conceal the consequences of her celestial relation with the prophet, out of her home."[39] Benjamin Johnson, a future patriarch of the Utah Mormon Church and brother of two of Joseph Smith's wives, testified that Fannie Alger was the Prophet's first plural wife.[40] Oliver Cowdery was furious with Joseph. When he would not back down in his criticism, Cowdery was excommunicated from the church. This pattern of infidelity and a wife's angry response was to be repeated many times in the stormy relationship between Emma and Joseph Smith.

These events occurred in secret. In the meantime, the Mormon colony at Kirtland experienced a period of relative prosperity. What most did not know at the time was that the prosperity was supported by mounting debt. Smith was in deep financial trouble. He was so deeply in debt by this time that he chose what could be described as desperate measures. He went on a treasure-hunting mission with his associates Sidney Rigdon, Oliver Cowdery, and Hyrum Smith to Salem, Massachusetts. Arriving in Salem in August, 1836, he stayed for a month. He received a new revelation that "I have much treasure in this city for you, for the benefit of Zion... wealth pertaining to gold and silver shall be yours. Concern not yourselves about your debts, for I will give you power to pay them."[41] Unfortunately for Joseph, this prophecy was never fulfilled in his lifetime. He arrived back in Kirtland in September with no treasure. This was the last of his known attempts at treasure-hunting.

Back in Missouri, the Mormons who had been forcibly removed from Jackson County began to settle down in Clay County to the north and east of Independence, in an area which came to be known as Far West, Missouri. The Missouri Mormons were desperately poor. They sent constant requests for financial help in order to acquire more land. The requests went unfulfilled. Rumblings began in Clay County that the non-Mormon residents wanted their unwelcome guests to move on.

Financial difficulty turned into disaster in Kirtland. In order to float his expanding debt, Joseph established the Kirtland Safety Society Bank Company in November 1837. The state of Ohio turned down their request to incorporate the bank. The bank was therefore illegal. Sidney Rigdon was president and Joseph Smith was cashier of the illegal operation. The bank began issuing worthless bank bills to pay off debt. This amounted to a kind of Ponzi scheme. The bank bills were not backed by any significant physical assets despite public claims to the contrary. Eventually, local non-Mormon merchants refused to accept the banknotes, and their value crashed. Joseph resigned his position, declaring disingenuously that the failure was due not to unethical practices, but to "the age of darkness, speculation and wickedness."[42] Many of the followers, who had given all their earthly property to Joseph on trust, found that their money had been used to pay off creditors. Six of the twelve apostles had already left the church, along with many others who had lost faith in the Prophet. When Smith went on a missionary trip to Canada in July, he returned to find that the church in Kirtland had split. David Whitmer, Martin Harris and Oliver Cowdery—the three witnesses—had all turned aside to follow a woman who claimed to see visions using a black stone to see the future. Joseph's return put this problem to an end, but Kirtland continued to fall apart. Many suits had been filed against him in the courts. He was repeatedly arrested, only to be bailed out by borrowed money.

*A Kirkland Bank Note—1837*

## Joseph Smith Escapes from Kirtland and Discovers the Garden of Eden

Clearly, fortune had turned against Joseph Smith in Ohio. He decided to quit Kirtland forever and pursue greener pastures in Missouri. Having heard of an ensuing arrest warrant for banking fraud, Joseph and Sidney Rigdon fled on horseback in the middle of the night in January 1838. They headed for the new Zion. Within hours, his precious temple in Kirtland was occupied by dissenters and Joseph was declared by his former followers to be depraved.

After a debacle on the order of that at Kirtland and the turning aside of most of his followers, a person of lesser self-confidence than Joseph Smith might have given up any grandiose plans. Joseph Smith was not this kind of man. By the time he reached Far West, a financial meltdown and ethical scandal had become God's means to bring him to "a more blessed and consecrated land." A city was mapped out on the prairie. The foundation for a grand temple was laid. With their usual optimism and zeal for hard work and industry, the Mormons staked out a city and spread out rapidly into the countryside, starting farms. Joseph went to scout out his Promised Land. On a bluff above the Grand River in Daviess County, followers found a small ruin which, to some, appeared to be an altar. Enthusiastic at this discovery, Joseph had a vision:

> Upon this very altar Adam himself offered up sacrifices to Jehovah. This place is Tower Hill, and at its feet we will lay out a city which shall be called Adam-on-di-Ahman. Here Adam, the Ancient of Days, shall come to visit his people. He shall sit on a throne of fiery flame, as predicted by Daniel the prophet, 'with thousand thousands ministering unto him and then thousand times ten thousand standing before him.[43]

Joseph declared that the area, including Far West, was the former site of the Garden of Eden. Here is one of many signs that Smith, like his followers, assigned a special place to America. The future of mankind revolved around what happened here and now, as it had in the distant past, and as it will in the glorious future to come. We see in this "vision" a nascent version of what became the Mormon doctrine that Adam was God. Smith claimed that Far West was the place where Cain killed Abel.[44] Did his followers at the time believe this invention? Presumably they did.

Not without reason, the Mormons, including Joseph Smith, feared for their safety, even though they were now at the very edge of white settlement. Up to this time, Joseph had generally insisted on peaceful means of defending the rights of his followers. In Far West he took a decisively different direction. It is at this time that Joseph, with the encouragement of Sidney Rigdon, began to form a secret militia. This group became known as the Danites. The shadowy organization was headed by Sampson Avard. The story of the Danites, their secret signs and passwords, as well as their murders and other criminal acts, are a serious blemish on the Mormon Church. Joseph gave his personal charge to the Danites:

> Know ye not, brethren, that it will soon be your privilege to take your respective companies and go out on a scout on the borders of the settlements, and take to yourselves spoils of the goods of the unbelievers?... and in this way we will build up the kingdom of God, and roll forth the little stone that Daniel was cut out of the mountain without hands and roll forth until it fills the earth.... I will swear a lie to clear any of you; and if this would not do, I would put them or him under the sand as Moses did the Egyptian; and in this way we will consecrate much unto the Lord.... And if one of this Danite Society reveals any of these things, I will put him where the dogs cannot bite him.[45]

This is a chilling testament to where the mind of Joseph Smith had turned by 1838. We see here the genesis of the name Danite (named after Daniel[46]), as well as the justification for lying to the "Gentiles" (non-Mormons) in order to defend the Latter-day Saints.

Not long after giving this address to the Danites, Joseph gave the following charge to his followers:

> If the people will let us alone, we will preach the gospel in peace. But if they come on us to molest us, we will establish our religion by the sword. We will trample down our enemies and make it one gore of blood from the Rocky Mountains to the Atlantic Ocean. I will be to this generation a second Mohammed, whose motto in treating for peace was, "the Alcoran or the Sword." So shall it eventually be with us—"Joseph Smith or the Sword!"[47]

We have already pointed out some obvious parallels between Joseph Smith and Muhammad. Both movements in time shifted from more peaceful tactics to the sword.

From this point, the end of Joseph's life was more or less set. The only remaining question was where and when his death would come.

## Joseph Smith in Jail and the Mormons Expelled from Missouri

The fall and winter of 1838–39 marked the end of the Mormon settlement in Far West. The Latter-day Saints were continuously harassed by the "old settlers" (non-Mormons) in Daviess County. Isolated farms were burned out. The refugees streamed into Far West. After repeated provocations, the Danites, under Sampson Avard and spurred on by Sidney Rigdon, finally went on the offensive. They organized nearly every adult male Mormon into the militia. Rigdon harangued the troops, "Now we as the people of God do declare and decree, by the Great Jehovah, the eternal and omnipotent God, that sits upon his vast and everlasting throne, beyond that ethereal blue, we will bathe our swords in the vital blood of the Missourians or die in the attempt."[48] A raiding party under Danite Lyman Wight attacked a number of settlements, bringing back booty to the starving Mormon settlers. These acts of the desperate followers of Joseph Smith are not easily defended. However, they pale in comparison to the brutal persecution brought on the Mormons by outsiders. The Governor of Missouri, Lilburn Boggs, issued a secret order to his militia that the Mormons should be exterminated or driven from the state. The most famous of the murderous attacks on the Mormons is known as the Haun's Mill massacre. In this incident 200 Missouri militia members attacked a small settlement, slaughtering eighteen defenseless settlers, including children. Hundreds were beaten in raids on the Mormon settlements by the state militia. Thousands were driven from their homes. Mormon women were raped.

Finally, Far West was surrounded by the militia, 6000 strong. The city was defended by 800 Mormon troops. Joseph Smith was forced to surrender himself and nearly all the leaders of his movement to arrest. Of the principle leaders, only Brigham Young escaped capture. While Smith and the other leaders of the movement languished in jail in Liberty, Missouri, Young organized the Mormons, cold and near starvation, to march across northern Missouri in the dead of winter. They were forced to give up all their property, their weapons and most of their possessions. They crossed into Illinois at Quincy. It is truly remarkable that the majority of the Mormon movement held together in this hour of physical peril, shame and degradation. The personal magnetism of Joseph Smith and the organizational skill of Brigham Young are the chief reasons they were able to survive this time as an organized movement.

In the meantime, Smith, Rigdon, and others barely escaped summary execution at the hands of their captors. Fortunately, calmer heads prevailed. With the exit of most of the Mormons from the state and the confiscation of their land and property, the immediate frenzy of the Missourians of Daviess County subsided. Smith, Rigdon, Parley Pratt, and others were put on trial in Richmond, Missouri on charges of treason, murder, arson, burglary, robbery, larceny and perjury. The judge heard the flimsy evidence against Smith. A number of apostates, including Sampson Avard, testified against Joseph Smith. Those who would defend the Mormons were intimidated into not testifying. Gradually, the true nature of the shameful treatment, including the land confiscations and the massacres of the Mormons, came out. With the Mormons leaving the state, the judge yielded to political expedience and released most of the arrested leaders. Only Smith and six others remained in jail. They were transferred to Liberty Jail, where they waited four months for their trial.

# Chapter 4

# The Final Stand in Nauvoo, Illinois

With the entrance of the Mormon sojourners into Illinois, we come to the final phase of the extraordinary life of Joseph Smith. It is in Nauvoo that Joseph reached his greatest influence as a religious leader. Here the prophet had his greatest (or his most outrageous) theological visions. Tens of thousands of admirers flocked to the New Zion on the prairie. For a brief period, Nauvoo, in Hancock County, was the largest city in Illinois. Here Smith reigned as a virtual king. However, it is also in western Illinois that he met his demise.

For those not familiar with the political relationship between Missouri and Illinois before the Civil War, it might be surprising to know that the followers of Joseph Smith were received with relatively open arms in Illinois. Illinois was a "free" state. There was no love lost between the Illini and the pro-slavery Missourians. By taking the Mormons into their state, the Illini shined a negative spotlight on the outrageous behavior of their despised neighbors in Missouri. The Democrats in Illinois were in a close political struggle with the Whigs. They hoped the Mormons would prove a reliable block of voters for their party. In the end, most residents of Illinois came to regret their decision to offer safe haven to the followers of Joseph Smith.

In the meantime, Joseph and friends awaited trial, having been transferred to Gallatin in Daviess County, Missouri. Because there was no way to get a jury of disinterested citizens in Daviess County, a change of venue was awarded to the defendants. On the way to Boone County, Joseph was met by supporters who offered a bribe of $800 to his jailer. The bribe was accepted and Smith made his escape. He quickly fled across the Mississippi River to join his followers in Nauvoo in April 1839.

Nauvoo was being built up rapidly. By early 1840 there were already more than 250 homes, laid out on well-ordered streets, with the foundation for a massive temple on the top of the central hill of the town. Two large steam sawmills were established. Plans were laid for a port on the Mississippi below Nauvoo. The Nauvoo Agricultural and Manufacturing Association was established. This association saw to the construction of a flour mill, an ironworks foundry, a chinaware factory and more. We see here the practical, hardworking ethic that has always characterized Mormon followers. They easily joined religion, the making of money and the practical affairs of life. They were nothing if not industrious. The willingness to cooperate and share resources with one another was a help to the economy of these settlers. Later on it was to be absolutely essential to their successful move to the Salt Lake Valley under Brigham Young.

In order to establish a secure position against the inevitable persecution, Smith needed numbers. He set his followers to missionary work both in the United States and overseas. In 1839 the twelve apostles all traveled to Europe. Mormonism was wildly successful among the disadvantaged industrial classes in England. Thousands were baptized into the new faith. Many of them pulled up stakes and moved to Nauvoo. By 1842 the population of Nauvoo, Illinois and the immediate surroundings grew to over 30,000. (General Joseph Smith speaks to his followers in Nauvoo, Illinois [above left].)

Events moved forward rapidly in Nauvoo. A shady character by the name of Dr. John Cook Bennett worked his way into favor with Joseph. He had political connections that secured for the Mormons a resolution in the Illinois senate known as the Nauvoo Charters. A young Abraham Lincoln gave his yes to the charters, as did his rival Stephen Douglas.

This victory gave to the Mormons almost complete autonomy in Nauvoo and to Smith unrivaled control of the economic, religious and political affairs of his followers. It gave him legal sanction to establish the Nauvoo Legion, with Joseph Smith as lieutenant general and Bennett as his brigadier general. The Nauvoo Legion grew to more than 2000 well-trained soldiers in 1841, and later, in 1843, to 4000. Smith felt this army was needed to protect him against the numerous attempts by the Missouri courts to arrest him. Not surprisingly, this made the neighboring non-Mormons nervous. The Nauvoo

Charters also authorized the establishment of Nauvoo University. By 1841, Bennett had replaced Sidney Rigdon as Smith's alter ego. Joseph was sufficiently enamored of Bennett's charms and political savvy that he was willing to ignore the negative revelation that Bennett had abandoned a wife and two children. He also had been banned from the Masons for unprincipled conduct.

It was at Nauvoo that Joseph Smith's theology was fully formed. It was also at this time that he produced the famous "Articles of Faith," which is an important Mormon creed and part of *The Pearl of Great Price*. And it was in Nauvoo that he began to speak publicly about the plurality of gods and that he established the vast array of elaborate temple rituals which are so characteristic of Mormonism today. Although Smith had already begun taking other women to himself sexually as early as Kirtland, it was at Nauvoo that he began to teach of the plurality of wives to his inner circle, and it was here that he took most of his plural "celestial wives."

## Masonry and Mormonism

The Book of Mormon was written in the late 1820s, during a time when the Freemasons were under much political and religious pressure. They were accused, probably falsely, of secretly plotting to overthrow the government of the United States. President Andrew Jackson was a high-level Mason and this became a political liability. Many churches demanded that their ministers denounce freemasonry or be fired. In such a climate, Joseph Smith wrote the Book of Mormon. Without naming the Masons, of course, he added thinly veiled denunciations of their system of secret rites and symbols in his book. He decried the "whoredoms" and "wickedness" of those who used "their secret signs, and their secret words; and this that they might distinguish a brother who had entered into the covenant, that whatsoever wickedness his brother should do, he should not be injured by his brother nor by those who did belong to his band, who had taken this covenant." (*Book of Mormon*, Heleman 6:22).

The political situation for the Freemasons had changed dramatically fifteen years later, when Joe Smith developed his well-known temple rituals. No longer did Joseph renounce the secret signs and symbols of the Masons, far from it. In fact, he became infatuated with their secret ceremonies. A Masonic temple was established in Nauvoo. The lodge met in Joseph's store. Joseph was a member of the Masonic Temple, rising to the "sublime degree" level within the hierarchy. John Bennett was the secretary of the lodge. Most of the Mormon leaders joined the secret society. Soon the lodge in Nauvoo was by far the largest group of the Masons in Illinois. Smith saw in the solemn ceremonies and secret rites of the Masons an ideal means to create a profound loyalty among the members of his rapidly growing movement. This is another example of his religious genius. At this point Mormonism became a mystery cult—with a ceremony almost identical to the Masons, but with parallels to the Gnostics, the Greek worshipers of Dionysus and others.

Just a few weeks after joining the Freemasons, Joseph called together his inner circle to announce the institution of "the ancient order of things for the first time in these last days."[49] What he gave them was an elaborate ritual that evolved into the famous but secret rituals performed in every Mormon temple across the world today. The ceremony was copied almost directly from Masonic ritual. Those to be incorporated into the "priesthood" of the Latter Day Saints were stripped naked and ritually washed and anointed in oil, after which they donned an unusual garment. The square and compass of the Masons was cut into the chest of the garment. A slash was opened in the abdomen, symbolic of the fact that they would be disemboweled if they revealed the secret of the ceremony to the uninitiated. This garment, thought to provide protection against the destroying angel, evolved into the secret underwear that all faithful Mormons wear today (except when they take part in sporting events for which the underwear would be too conspicuous).

The initiates then changed into a white garment. They witnessed as a group a ritual play which was an allegory of the creation of Adam and Eve and their temptation by the serpent. After viewing the drama, initiates were given a number of Mason-like secret handshakes and other "keys," as well as a secret name, to be known only by them, which would be their name in the kingdom of heaven.

*The Nauvoo Temple*

How did Smith explain to his leaders the blatant incorporation of the Masonic symbols, including the all-seeing eye, the beehive, handshakes, symbols and dramatic allegory, into his temple ceremony? It was impossible for them to miss the fact that Mormonism was swallowing Masonic practice almost whole. His explanation was that the Masonic ritual was a corruption of that handed down by Solomon and that the version he gave to them was a restoration of the original Jewish ceremony. Apparently, Joseph's power of persuasion was sufficient for his followers to accept this far-fetched explanation. We will have more to say in chapter eight about these unusual rites performed in Mormon temples.

## Joseph Smith, Polygamy and Polyandry

As already mentioned, it was in Kirtland that Joseph Smith began to take advantage of Mormon women other than his legal wife, Emma. Having tasted the fruit of his seemingly unlimited power over women in Nauvoo, Joseph abandoned all reason in this regard. The actual number of women he took in celestial marriage is unknown. How many of these "marriages" were consummated is also in doubt. What is not in doubt is that Smith's behavior with women in his movement was unsavory.

Fawn M. Brodie[50] conservatively documents forty-eight wives taken by Joseph Smith. His information comes from Mormon documents such as the Nauvoo Temple, at which Smith was sealed "for eternity" to thirty women. Other reliable sources list as many as sixty-seven women who were sealed to Joseph while he was still alive.[51] Some he married "for time"—a euphemism for marriages which most likely were consummated. Others he married "for eternity"—a euphemism for relationships that were more likely not consummated. Brigham Young claimed to have joined Joseph to dozens of women.[52] Many of them—at least a dozen—were still married to other male members of the Mormon movement when they began their sexual relationship with Smith. This makes Smith not only a polygamist but also one who took part in polyandry (when a woman has more than one husband). The youngest well-documented wife of Smith whose "marriage" was almost certainly consummated was Helen Mar Kimball. She was fifteen when she was asked by her father Heber C. Kimball to marry Kimball's religious leader—thirty-eight-year-old Joseph Smith. To quote from Helen,

> "[My father] asked me if I would be sealed to Joseph... [Smith] said to me, 'If you will take this step, it will ensure your eternal salvation and exaltation and that of your father's household and all of your kindred. This promise was so great that I willingly gave myself to purchase so glorious a reward. ... [After the marriage] I felt quite sore over it... and thought myself an abused child, and that it was pardonable if I did murmur."[53]

Rather than go into any more of the sordid details, numbers or names, we will let this single example of what could be described as abuse of women represent the rest of Smith's polygamous activities.

This behavior was not only illegal, but also outrageous. For a person who claims to be a spiritual leader of a "Christian" group to give total abandon to his sexual desire is inexcusable. How many marriages did he ruin? How many men left his movement in disgust because of his unbridled desire? How many young girls lost their innocence to the sexual appetite of Joseph Smith? By 1842, Brigham Young, Hyrum Smith, Heber C. Kimball and many others were taking multiple "celestial wives." This assured Smith that his closest associates would not expose him publicly, as many of his confidantes were guilty of the same behavior.

In order to justify behavior which he had already taken part in, Joseph Smith claimed to have a revelation, giving inspired support to his promiscuity. One of his revelations concerning plural wives is found in *Doctrine and Covenants*, Section 132.

> Verily, thus saith the Lord unto my servant Joseph that inasmuch as you have inquired of my hand to know and understand wherein I, the Lord justified my servants Abraham, Isaac and Jacob, as also Moses, David and Solomon my servants, as touching the principle and doctrine of their having many wives and concubines...

Here Smith has God saying that not only is polygamy permitted, but also it is actually a means by which Abraham, Isaac, Jacob, Moses, David and Solomon were justified. According to the Bible, Abraham was justified by his faith, not by his polygamy (Romans 4:1, quoting Genesis 15:6). How Mormons today are to be justified now that polygamy has been disavowed by the Utah Mormons is also unclear. Polygamy is, after all, named a "new and everlasting covenant."[54] Those men who take plural wives are given greater rewards in heaven.[55] Polygamists are promised that "then they shall be called gods because they have all power and the angels are subject unto them." The revelation included the encouragement to polygamists that, "..if he have ten virgins given unto him by this law, he cannot commit adultery, for they belong to him."[56] Poor Emma Smith was threatened in the same revelation: "But if she will not abide this commandment, she will be destroyed, saith the Lord." When Joseph's brother Hyrum agreed to the dubious job of revealing this new revelation to Emma, he reported back to Joseph that he had never been so abused by a woman. Smith replied, "I told you, you didn't know Emma as well as I did."[58]

At first Joseph only revealed his revelation concerning polygamy to his inner circle. Polygamy was not openly taught to the entire movement until 1852, once the Mormons were safely established in isolated Utah. During his lifetime, Joseph Smith continued to deny that polygamy was practiced in his church. He inserted a disclaimer into the 1835 edition of *Doctrine and Covenants* in which he responded to the claims of "fornication and polygamy" in his church, that "we declare that we believe that one man should have one wife and one woman but one husband." He repeated this public lie many times in Far West and in Nauvoo.

## Joseph Smith Writes His Own History

Joseph set about to write his autobiography beginning in 1841, under the title *History of the Church of Jesus Christ of Latter-Day Saints*. This was both an interpretation of his life for the sake of his followers and a personal account of the growth of the Mormon movement. In *History of the Church* Joseph Smith said about himself: "I was ordained from before the foundation of the world, for some good end, or bad...But, nevertheless, deep water is what I am wont to swim in; it has all become second nature to me."[59] Although most of this history is not part of the official scripture of Mormonism (a small portion is in the *Pearl of Great Price*), it is used widely by the Mormon Church today. It is both a source of historical information on the life of Smith and a source of insight into how Joseph created his public persona.

## Joseph Breaks with John Cook Bennett

In the first half of 1842 Smith's relationship with John Bennett came to a turbulent end. Bennett had used his position as favorite of Smith and as midwifery instructor to the Mormons in Nauvoo in order to gain many sexual partners. Bennett began to publicly preach "promiscuous intercourse." His open espousal of what was happening behind closed doors made him a major liability, especially as he was well acquainted with Smith's still-secret celestial marriages. Further magnifying the liability he posed, Bennett was mayor of Nauvoo.

To get rid of this trouble, Joseph produced a number of affidavits about Bennett's sexual encounters. Bennett was excommunicated on June 23, 1842, at which time Joseph publicly exposed his misdeeds. Bennett retaliated by publishing a number of letters exposing the sexual exploits of the principal Mormon leaders, as well as the violent behavior of the Danites. He accused Smith of trying to overthrow the governments in the Western states. We can assume that many of the charges were exaggerated or perhaps even made up completely, but some of the actions with which he charged "Joe Smith" are well documented elsewhere. These letters were published in newspapers throughout the United States. Ultimately, the Mormon hierarchy was able to utterly discredit the self-serving Bennett within the Mormon community, but the effect of exposing the licentious behavior in the Mormon leaders, especially Smith, was irreversible. It became just a matter of time before the non-Mormon residents of Illinois would do to the Mormons what their neighbors in Missouri had done in Far West.

It did not improve the public opinion of Smith when former Governor Boggs of Missouri was found shot in May 1842. Smith had made public statements in the spring of 1841 about Boggs that were interpreted at the time as a threat against his life. The Whig papers openly implied that Joseph orchestrated the murder of his enemy. Joseph, of course, denied the charges. His denials may have been sincere, but still the incident did not help his public perception. Miraculously, Boggs survived the attack. The irrepressible John Bennett visited Boggs. He corroborated the accusations against Smith and implicated a certain Porter Rockwell, an associate of Joseph Smith, for the attempted murder. Boggs was able to convince Governor Carlin of Missouri to issue an arrest warrant for Joseph and Rockwell. The warrant was served in Nauvoo, but Smith was able to get a writ of *habeas corpus*, freeing him from arrest. Smith went into hiding, well aware that to be taken to Missouri under arrest meant his possible execution.

After four months in hiding, Joseph decided to submit to arrest in Illinois rather than face continued harassment from the Missouri sheriffs who lurked in Nauvoo. He traveled to Springfield with forty of his soldiers for protection. In Springfield, his amiable character won over his enemies in the Illinois State house. The judge rendered the arrest warrant from Missouri invalid in Illinois, and Joseph went free.

For a few months, Joseph enjoyed relative freedom of movement, but his enemies John Bennett and Lilburn Boggs continued to plot how to destroy him from across the Mississippi River in Missouri. They obtained a fresh arrest warrant for treason in May 1843. They crossed to Illinois to make good the arrest. Stalking Smith, they kidnapped him at gunpoint as he traveled from a meeting. Their efforts were foiled, however, by Whig politicians who in turn had the sheriffs from Missouri arrested for assault and false imprisonment. Smith was scheduled to appear before Judge Stephen A. Douglas in Quincy, Illinois. (This is the same Douglas whose debates with Abraham Lincoln fifteen years later impelled the younger Abe to the presidency.) Because of a prior agreement, Smith was confident of being released by Douglas. On their way to Quincy with the Missouri sheriffs for trial, the party was overcome by 140 members of the Mormon Militia. Relieved to have escaped death in Missouri, Smith declared, "These are my boys!" He was received with joy by a crowd of 10,000 in Nauvoo. In an exultant speech to the crowd, he declared, "If mobs come upon you any more here, dung your gardens with them." In his own city, he was issued another writ of *habeas corpus*. However, it turned out later that because this was not a state court, the order was overturned. This led to grave consequences for Smith.

## Joseph Smith, Politician

The Mormons had political ambitions in the state of Illinois. Joseph's brother

William was already in the state legislature. His more famous brother Hyrum had promised the Mormon vote for governor in 1843 to the Democrats in return for being given a seat of his own in the Illinois house. Hyrum duly announced a revelation that all the Mormons should support the Democratic candidate Hoge for the Illinois legislature. This blunder gave the election to Hoge but turned the Whigs from being strong allies of the Mormon movement to avowed enemies.

Joseph's unbridled ambition shifted from local politics to the national theatre. In December 1843 he drafted a petition to the US Congress demanding that Nauvoo be granted status as a completely independent federal territory, and his Nauvoo Legion declared a part of the US Army. When this demand was published it destroyed whatever political support the Mormons had in the state of Illinois. Smith said, "I prophesied by virtue of the holy Priesthood vested in me, and in the name of the Lord Jesus Christ, that, if Congress will not hear our petition and grant us protection, they shall be broken up as a government and God shall damn them, and there shall be nothing left of them—not even a grease spot!"[60] In March 1844 Smith secretly set up a council of fifty "princes" to govern an eventual independent Mormon state. They secretly appointed Smith "King of the Kingdom of God"—a position reserved to Jesus Christ in biblical Christianity. At this point, the only likely end for the movement seemed to be the death of its leader and the scattering of its members, or the emigration of the Mormons to points outside the occupied territory of the United States. Smith began to make preparations for the latter option. Discussions began between the Council of Fifty and the government of what was at that time the independent nation of Texas for a move to a proposed autonomous Mormon territory in Texas.

Paradoxically, while plotting against the US government, Smith decided to run for the presidency. In the spring, he entered the lists for the 1844 election. His followers began to go out on the stump supporting their candidate. Smith obviously knew he could not win a national election, but he hoped to gain respect for his movement and to gain enough votes to be a kind of power broker over the established Whig and Democratic parties. Smith's choice for vice president was Sidney Rigdon. Smith appeared to be riding a wave of success. In a moment of supreme self-confidence, Smith delivered perhaps his most famous public sermon, on April 7, 1844. This is the one in which he publicly announced the doctrine he had long been contemplating, the plurality of gods. We will soon hear more of this doctrine.

## The Road to Carthage

We might have expected that the events which led to the arrest and death of Joseph Smith would have come from outside the Mormon movement. This is not the case.

A prominent and wealthy Mormon convert named William Law became disillusioned with his spiritual leader. His disaffection was over moral issues—especially the plural wife practice—and because of Smith's nearly complete monopoly over financial matters in the Nauvoo area. Rather than taking the approach of the hotheaded John Bennett by publicly denouncing Smith, he chose to work from within to bring about reform, hoping Smith would see the light and repent of his immoral behavior. For William Law, the straw that broke the camel's back was learning that Smith had attempted to seduce his wife, Jane, to enter into a plural marriage. According to his own account, a furious William Law confronted Smith, demanding that if he did not repent and confess before the High Council, he would publicly expose his seductions. Smith refused, pointing out to his new found enemy that, "I'll be damned before I do. If I admitted to the charges you would heap upon me, it would prove the overthrow of the Church!"[61]

Having split with Smith, but still thinking of reforming the movement, Law began a periodical titled the *Nauvoo Expositor*. He published expositions against polygamy, as well as criticizing Smith's land speculation, his use of religion to gain political power, his abuse of the Nauvoo Charters and more. In response, Smith first publicly attacked the character of Law and his associates, but when that did not have the desired effect, he made the disastrous mistake of declaring the *Expositor* a public menace. A detachment of the Nauvoo Legion was dispatched to destroy the press and burn every extant copy of the newspaper. It was this action that set in motion the now-famous shoot-out in Carthage, Illinois.

## The Carthage Jail

Upon hearing of the burning of the *Expositor* by the Nauvoo Militia, Illinois Governor Thomas Ford traveled to Carthage to initiate an investigation. He found that the Carthage and the nearby Warsaw militia had already been called up. He asked Joseph Smith and the other perpetrators of the crime to voluntarily submit to arrest. Joseph replied that he would submit to arrest in Carthage, but demanded that he be escorted there by the Nauvoo Militia. He told Ford that he feared a lynching—a fear not without foundation. Afraid of a civil war and the destruction of Nauvoo, Governor Ford refused this request. Smith fled the law by a midnight crossing of the Mississippi at flood stage in a rowboat.

At the home of a trusted follower in Iowa, Smith contemplated his fate. He was unprepared to flee into the wilderness, but, as he said to his brother Hyrum about his capture by the Illinois authorities, "Just as sure as we fall into their hands, we are dead men." In a letter, Emma pleaded with him to come back and defend his people. Finally, Joseph re-crossed the Mississippi. On June 24, 1844, at the age of thirty-eight, Joseph set out for Carthage, with his brother Hyrum and a small entourage, to turn himself in to the authorities under the promised protection of Governor Ford.

In Carthage, Joseph and Hyrum were charged with treason on the grounds that they had called up the Nauvoo Militia to thwart the Illinois posse sent to arrest them. They were incarcerated in the Carthage jail. Governor Ford came to visit Joseph in his cell. They agreed that the only legitimate charge on the table was the destruction of the opposition press. In the meantime, members of the local militias were plotting to storm the jail and kill Smith as soon as Governor Ford left.

This is exactly what happened. Immediately after the governor left Carthage for Nauvoo, on June 27, a mob of militia shot their way into the jail. Joseph and Hyrum both had pistols that had been smuggled in to them by supporters. A gunfight ensued. Hyrum was killed almost immediately. Joseph fired all six shots from his pistol, wounding at least one of the mob seriously. A hail of bullets finally struck Joseph, and he fell from the jail window. At this point Colonel Williams ordered the men to fire on the wounded and unarmed Smith. Joseph was dispatched by this cowardly act. The deed complete, the militia fled. Thus the life of the self-proclaimed prophet came to an end.

## Summary analysis of the life of Joseph Smith

No matter how we feel about Joseph Smith, it is impossible to defend the way he and his brother Hyrum were murdered by the mob in Carthage. The fact that the brothers were armed does little to lessen the shame of the residents of Illinois. Unwittingly, by this public action they had created a martyr.

Was Joseph Smith a true martyr—killed as the result of religious persecution? That is what the Mormon Church would have us believe. Whether he was killed for religious reasons is debatable. The evidence leads to the conclusion that he was assassinated principally for political reasons. The motivation of the crowd was fear. This fear was caused by a number of political acts on the part of Joseph. These acts included his call for an independent federal state for the Mormons within Illinois, as well as his run for the presidency of the United States. The non-Mormons were fearful of his unrivaled power in Nauvoo and his possession of a personal militia of over 4000 armed soldiers. Moral outrage over his religious pretensions were a secondary cause of his murder.

How are we to view the man Joseph Smith? He was a supremely talented person. In some ways he could be thought of as a great man. He had an uncanny ability to inspire people with his personal vision. Although his energies were devoted to building his own public persona, he was paradoxically capable of great self-sacrifice. He had a unique ability to give unity and purpose to people from all levels of society. He could inspire incredible loyalty. He had a great practical sense and understood what motivated people. He was able to keep his head when all around him were panicking. Repeatedly, when pressured by his followers to resort to the open use of violence against his enemies, he refused to take this path.

Yet, Joseph did have deep character flaws. On balance, there is no question that his flaws outweighed his strengths. Smith seemed incapable of distinguishing truth from deception. He was a man of hubris. He had an irrational sense of his own abilities and importance. His passion was unbridled. His passion and hubris came together in his unconscionable treatment of emotionally vulnerable women and the destruction of of a number of marriages. He used deception to convince many to give all their worldly possessions to his cause.

In the final analysis, Smith does not deserve to be considered a prophet and certainly not a man of God. He did not deliver on his promise to take his people to the Promised Land. His vision was a lie. His claim to speak for God was presumptuous in the extreme, and it was certainly fraudulent.

As already stated, the typical Mormon witness begins with the statement: "This is my testimony, Joseph Smith is a Prophet." This testimony cannot be supported by the evidence, both within Mormonism and from his public life. He was a man of great talent, no doubt, but his abilities were overshadowed by a deeply flawed moral character. To many he was considered a dangerous man. He was not a prophet of God.

# Chapter 5

# A Shattered Movement Finds a New Leader and a New Home in the West

The leader of the Mormon movement lay dead outside a jail in Carthage, Illinois. What was to happen to the Latter Day Saints, now that their leader and prophet was dead? The book of Acts offers a perspective on dynamic religious movements led by a charismatic man. When asked for advice concerning what to do with the young Jesus movement, the greatest rabbi of the age, Gamaliel, pointed out that both Theudas and Judas the Galilean had attracted large followings, but when they died, their followers were scattered and their movements ended. He advised the Jews to let the Jesus movement go the way of most human-inspired movements. "If their purpose or activity is of human origin, it will fail" (Acts 5:38). Once the leader has left the scene, the followers will scatter like dust in the wind. Cut off the head and the body will perish. Christians find this wise advice by Gamaliel to be ironic, as we understand Jesus' movement to be of divine, not human origin, and we know that his movement definitely did not die after he left the scene.

Reason and experience predict this is exactly what would happen to the followers of Joseph Smith. Certainly this is what the enemies of the Latter-day Saints hoped would be the result of dispatching the leader of the Mormons. Surely his work was of human, not godly origin. By Gamaliel's logic, we could predict that the movement would scatter. An editorial appeared in the *New York Herald* on the death of the prophet on July 8, 1844:

> "The death of the modern Mahomet will seal the fate of Mormonism. They cannot get another Joseph Smith. The holy city must tumble into ruins, and the 'latter day saints' have indeed come to the latter day."

However, this is not what happened to the Latter-day Saints. After a brief period of chaos, during which it appeared that the followers of Smith would, indeed, be scattered to the winds, a visionary leader with an iron will arose. The mantle of the Mormon leadership fell to Brigham Young. This chapter is the story of the remarkable turn of events that brought the bulk of the followers of Joseph Smith to the Great Basin in Utah under the leadership of Brigham Young. The trek of the Mormon pioneers across more than 1000 miles of wilderness and their successful colonization of the Salt Lake Valley is one of the most fascinating sagas in American history. This chapter is also the story of how Young left his imprint on the organization and the theology of the Mormon religion.

## From Nauvoo, Illinois to Winter Quarters

Joseph Smith's body was brought from Carthage to Nauvoo. An estimated 20,000 mourners viewed his body as it lay in state. With Joseph dead, the Warsaw militia, which had assassinated him, scattered. The Nauvoo legion pledged to avenge the blood of the "martyrs," but with time, cooler heads prevailed. All twelve of the Mormon apostles were away from Nauvoo on various missions at the time. In the immediate aftermath, several of Joseph Smith's influential leaders tried to claim the mantle of Prophet to the Latter-day Saints. Sidney Rigdon hurried back from Pittsburgh to Nauvoo in hopes of being declared the next Prophet. He tried to hurry through an election at a hastily called convention of Mormon leaders. Brigham Young arrived on August 6. The convention was to be held on the eighth. Rigdon tried to claim the presidency of the church. Wisely, Brigham deferred to the twelve apostles. "I say unto you that the Quorum of the Twelve have the keys to the kingdom of God in all the world."[62] Having given them the formal power to lead the church, the twelve returned the favor and made Brigham Young, effectively the autocratic leader of the saints who remained in Nauvoo. They declared him "The Lion of the Lord."

Sidney Rigdon attempted to gather a faction around himself in Pittsburgh. He formed his own group of twelve apostles. In his periodical, *The Latter Day Saints' Messenger and Advocate,* he denounced the Nauvoo Mormons under Young for "practicing the doctrine of polygamy, despoiling female virtue and chastity by seducing them, and tyrannizing over those who will not sanction their work of darkness, and many other like things, for which we regard them as apostates." In the end, Rigdon was an emotionally unstable man, and his faction soon evaporated.

A more significant group of the scattered saints grew up around James J. Strang. Strang produced a letter he claimed to have been written by Joseph Smith, postmarked from Nauvoo on June 19, 1844. The letter directed Strang to plant a stake of Zion in Voree, Wisconsin, urging all the saints to join him there. This letter, or at least part of it, was probably a forgery.[63] Strang claimed visions suspiciously similar to those of Joseph Smith, even digging up an account of an ancient extinct people, recorded on plates in a language only Strang knew. By 1846 the Strangites grew to 10,000, while the followers of the sect under Brigham Young were somewhat greater than 15,000.[64] William Smith, Joseph's brother, as well as original witness Martin Harris and many others, joined this group for a time. After 1850, membership in the Strangite group fell sharply when Strang publicly embraced polygamy. His earlier rejection of this teaching was one of the reasons many disaffected from Young's faction had followed Strang. In 1860, he was shot in the back and his remaining followers were dispersed.

A smaller but more enduring Mormon sect grew around the church patriarch William Smith and his nephew, Joseph's oldest son, Joseph Smith III. William was the last living brother of Joseph Smith. Many witnesses claimed that Joseph had repeatedly stated his son would succeed him. The *Doctrine and Covenants*[63] made it clear that the priesthood was hereditary. However, Brigham Young soon alienated William, who called Brigham "a Pontius Pilate." William complained, "I say of this B. Young, no greater tyranny ever existed since the days of Nero."[66] Brigham alienated Emma Smith as well. Not surprisingly, she did not accept his request to marry him. She maintained a lifelong enmity toward Young. Eventually, Brigham drove William Smith out of Nauvoo. William and young Joseph III supported the Strangites for a time. Later, they broke with Strang when he came out in favor of plural marriage. In April 1860, Joseph Smith III was announced as prophet, seer and revelator of what became the Reorganized Church of Jesus Christ of Latter-day Saints. The "Josephites" condemned the doctrines of Brigham Young. In practice and teaching the Reorganized Mormons resembled the Utah sect, with the principle exceptions being their renunciation of polygamy and of the presidency of Brigham Young. The group exists to this day, centered in Independence, Missouri. They occupy the land on which Joseph had declared that the modern-day Zion would be established. This Mormon sect recently changed their name to the Community of Christ. They number about 250,000 members worldwide.

Meanwhile, the situation became tenuous for the Nauvoo Mormons under Brigham Young. The Nauvoo Charters were repealed in 1845. This ended the Mormon monopoly of power in Nauvoo. Anti-Mormon pressure grew on the church—reminiscent of Missouri in 1839—to the point that it became clear they must leave Nauvoo or be suppressed by means legal or illegal. One hundred and fifty Mormon homes had already been burned by October 1845. To make matters more difficult, Brigham was indicted in December on charges of counterfeiting. A federal posse sought to arrest Young on these charges. Brigham reached the momentous decision to move his followers to a place where they truly could practice their version of latter-day Christianity without fear of reprisals from locals who could not accept polygamy and Mormon exclusivism. The question became not if they were to leave, but *where* should they go. Joseph was already anticipating this move before he was killed. He had considered moving his group to Texas, to Oregon, or to Arkansas.

But even these places already had settlers. Brigham Young wanted a space where there was no competition whatsoever from non-Mormons for land or political power. Even if only a small remnant could be brought to a new Zion, Young reasoned that he could build from that core. By the second half of the 1840s the rush to Oregon and California had already begun. To the casual observer, the choice of the Salt Lake Valley may seem a fit of insanity. It was in the middle of a huge desert, more than 1000 miles from Nauvoo, surrounded by hostile Indian groups. However, we should assume that Brigham Young was a very smart man. If one looks at a map of the western United States, searching for the best location between the Rockies and the western mountain ranges to establish a colony to farm the land, the obvious choice is the valley around the Great Salt Lake. Although the climate in the area is dry, there are dozens of streams which exit the Rocky Mountains into the valley, providing a year-round source of water. The climate is relatively mild and the soil is of good quality. Young had read positive stories about the valley from Lieutenant John C. Fremont's journal as early as 1845. Fremont described the Salt Lake Valley as fertile and well watered. In any case, Young reached his decision in late 1845 and the die was cast.

In February 1846, two thousand Mormons crossed from Nauvoo into Iowa. Stubborn to the end, even knowing that they were leaving Nauvoo, Brigham saw to near-completion the building of the Nauvoo Temple. As the leaders prepared to flee the city, the upper level of the temple was consecrated. Brigham Young was "sealed" to thirty-four of his wives in a brief ceremony in the temple that was abandoned just a few days later. Eight of these wives were widows of Joseph Smith. One of the wives was Rhoda Richards, Young's first cousin.

The Mormons traveled in wagons past the farthest point of settlement in Iowa, crossing into Nebraska Territory. Twelve thousand settlers were scattered between Nauvoo and the vanguard. Young decided to establish a settlement in Nebraska, on the Platte River, near modern-day Omaha. The settlement became known as Winter Quarters. The suffering of the Mormon pilgrims is the stuff of LDS legend. Hundreds died of disease and starvation on the trail to Utah. In Winter Quarters, Young set up a temporary settlement, with as many as 1000 homes. However, the intention all along was to proceed west. In the spring of 1847 a ragged group of settlers headed out of Nebraska, through Wyoming, on what became known as the Mormon Trail.

## Brigham Young: His Youth, Conversion and Rise to Leadership of the Mormon Movement

With the bulk of the remaining Latter-day Saints about to enter the Great Basin under the leadership of Brigham Young, let us turn to the life of this remarkable man. The description of his biographer Stanley P. Hirshson does him justice:

> Brigham Young was a marvel of his age: the husband of seventy wives, the father of fifty-six children, the colonizer of vast areas of the West, the Yankee prophet of God, the Moses of the modern children of Israel, the religious imperialist bent on conquering the world. Gentiles or non-Mormons labeled him a fraud, a dictator, and a murderer. His followers revered him, obeyed his every command and believed he alone would determine whether they spent eternity in heaven or hell.[67]

Brigham Young was born, the fourth son and ninth child of John and Nabby Young, on June 1, 1801 in Whitingham, Vermont. He was four years older than his future religious mentor Joseph Smith. Brigham's mother was deeply religious. Young said that she constantly reminded him to reverence the Bible: "Read it, observe its precepts and apply them to your lives as far as you can."[68] John Young was a farmer and, reportedly, not a very successful one. He moved the family to Sherburne, in Chenango County, New York in 1804. Not finding fortune there, he moved on to farm in Tyrone, New York in 1812. Young Brigham had a total of eleven days of formal education in his formative years. He reached adulthood completely unable to read or write.

In 1815, Brigham's mother, Nabby, died. The large Young family broke up at the time. At fourteen years of age, Brigham was forced to move from place to place, working for room and board only. One thing that separates Brigham Young from Joseph Smith is that he was not averse to hard physical work. In 1823 he met his future wife,

Miriam Works. Twenty-three-year-old Brigham married seventeen-year-old Miriam on October 8, 1824. By this time Brigham was already a large and physically powerful man. By all reports he was very handsome and irresistibly attractive to many women.

In 1829, Young moved to Mendon, New York with his wife and three-year-old daughter. His father and much of his family had come together in Mendon. Here his interest in religion grew. Three of Brigham's older brothers were itinerant preachers for the Methodist Episcopal Reformed Church. Also important for his future leadership, it was here that Young met his lifelong friend and supporter Heber C. Kimball. Both of them first heard of the new prophet and seer Joseph Smith and his Golden Book in 1831. According to Kimball, he and Brigham were out chopping wood together when they heard loud shouts and screams, "...and we did shout aloud, 'Hosannah to God and the Lamb.'"[69] Moved by their religious experience, both Heber Kimball and Brigham Young joined the young Mormon movement. Young was baptized into the church on April 15, 1832. He was ordained an elder of the church "before my clothes were dry upon me."[70] Brigham never looked back.

Miriam died just five months after her husband's conversion, in September 1832. Soon after losing his wife, Brigham made a pilgrimage to Kirtland, Ohio to meet Smith and his followers. On the way to Kirtland, Brigham met with a critic of the young movement who warned him against the money-digger and horse thief, Joe Smith. According to Young, his reply to the wise words of the one he met on the road was to share his witness about Joseph Smith:

> He says that he has received revelations from God, and declared that an angel visited him. He has declared that he found plates, and other witnesses have seen and handled them, from which the Book of Mormon was translated. I know nothing about the witnesses, nor do I care. I went to my Father in heaven and asked with regard to the truth of the doctrines taught by Joseph Smith, and I know that they will save all that will hearken to them, and that those who do not will miss salvation in the celestial kingdom of God; and though Joseph Smith should steal horses every day, or gamble every night, or deny his Savior from the crowing of the cock in the morning until the sunset in the evening, I know that the doctrine he preaches is the power of God to my salvation, if I live it. I did not make him a revelator; I have no business to dictate to him."[71]

Here Brigham is probably reading his thoughts at a later time back into the event on the road to Kirtland. In any case, with this quote we catch a glimpse of why Mormons tend to be immune to rational argument about their religious experiences. For them it is the testimony, not the facts, evidence or reasoning which determines truth.

We have already seen how his first meeting with Joseph Smith went. Joseph recognized Brigham's potential immediately, giving the stamp of approval to his speaking in tongues, calling it a pure Adamic language. Soon, Brigham became one of Joseph Smith's closest and most loyal allies. From the time he arrived in Kirtland until his death, Young was Joseph's most steady and reliable supporter. In 1835, when Joseph appointed his twelve apostles, Brigham Young and Heber Kimball were chosen second and third for the honor.

Young remarried on March 31, 1834, to Mary Ann Angell. Soon, events in far-off Independence, Missouri called Brigham to leave his wife behind. He traveled with the two hundred of Zion's Camp to aid the persecuted Mormons in the West. After the disastrous end of this affair, Young returned to Kirtland where he faced the financial fiasco of the collapse of Kirtland Safety Society Bank. Young fled Kirtland with Smith and Sidney Rigdon on the fastest horses they could find. Ever the loyal supporter, Young later ably led the Mormons in Far West while Joseph lay in prison in Daviess County, Missouri. As a foreshadow of his bringing the Mormons to Utah, Brigham was the only one of the Mormon leaders both free from prison and possessing the leadership qualities and level-headedness to guide the Mormons in an orderly way out of Far West. They were under constant threat of massacre by their enemies. In the dead of winter, he led them across the Mississippi to form the settlement at Nauvoo, Illinois. Only Young's iron will and steadfast faith in his prophet could have held the Saints together during this incredibly challenging period in the Mormon saga. In Nauvoo, Brigham's star continued to rise as Sidney Rigdon proved an unstable leader and many of the earlier witnesses and apostles proved to be less reliable as well. Still sick from malaria, Brigham made a grueling missionary trip along with Spencer Kimball from September 1839 to July 1841. They evangelized in New England, New York and England. Young arrived in England with seventy-five cents in his pocket. The campaign was wildly successful. Thousands were baptized and a flood of immigrants headed across the Atlantic to join the prophet at Nauvoo.

Upon Brigham's return to Nauvoo, Joseph informed his close confidant that he was restoring the teaching of plural marriage. We should probably take Young at his word that he was initially repelled by this revelation. However, as with all other matters, Brigham fell in line with his "revelator," Joseph Smith. "I plainly saw the great trials and abuse of it [of plural marriages] that would be made by many of the Elders, and the trouble and persecution that it would bring upon this whole people. But the Lord revealed it, and it was my business to accept it."[72] He later became perhaps the most vocal supporter of celestial marriage. By 1844, Young had taken at least four celestial wives. He fell in love with Lucy Decker, even though she was already married to Isaac Seely, a Nauvoo doctor. While Isaac was out of town, Young asked the high council of the church to annul Isaac's marriage to Lucy. On June 1842, forty-one-year-old Brigham married the twenty-year-old Lucy, taking her two children from Isaac as well. We can only imagine how Isaac Decker felt about this decision. In 1844, Brigham married Lucy's fourteen-year-old sister as well. He was more than three times her age at the time. We will spare the reader most of the shocking details of the many marriages of Brigham Young, and the destroyed families left in his wake. Biographer Stanley Hirshson documents seventy wives and fifty-six children of the energetic Mr. Young.[73]

With his strong work ethic, his willingness to make personal sacrifice, his unquestioning loyalty, levelheadedness, political acumen, and incorruptibility with regard to financial matters, it is no wonder that Brigham Young quickly became the consensus choice of the twelve apostles to succeed Joseph Smith on his death. No one in the inner circle was even a close second.

## The Mormons Reach Salt Lake

Now that the Mormon leader has received a proper introduction, let us return to the Mormon host as they enter into their new Zion—their Deseret in the wilderness. (The Mormons gave the name Deseret to their home in the Salt Lake Valley. They

*A lithograph of early Salt Lake City, circa 1848*

claimed, falsely, that the word comes from the Egyptian word for honeybee. Salt Lake was their Promised Land—their land of milk and honey. When they declared themselves a de facto state, they called themselves the State of Deseret. To this day, the beehive is the state symbol in Utah, and is found on all their state highway signs). On July 2, 1847, the first group of Mormon immigrants entered the depression around the Salt Lake. Within a week, the pioneers had selected the site which became the center of Salt Lake City, laid out a street grid for the city, dammed a creek leading to the Great Salt Lake, and planted five acres of potatoes. In what has always been a mark of Mormon culture, the followers of Joseph Smith immediately went to work.

Mormon lore is full of stories of the miraculous way those who followed Brigham Young brought the desert to bloom and overcame impossible odds to carve out their state of Deseret. They recount with pride the story of the plague of locusts that were devastating their crops, and the "miraculous" appearance of sea gulls to destroy the locusts and save the crop (actually sea gulls are native to the Great Salt Lake area, making this "miracle" a natural phenomenon). Whether or not miracles happened is questionable. The fact remains that it was the wise and steady leadership of Brigham Young that was the chief factor in the willingness of the followers of Joseph Smith to endure severe hardship to reach the new Zion. Their industriousness and spirit of cooperation allowed them to accomplish a feat of settlement in untracked wilderness without precedent in the history of the United States. (Though it should be noted that from 1847 to 1849, Utah was still a part of Mexico).

What gave the Saints the determination to make this incredible trek into the virtual unknown? Clearly, part of the motivation was the sincere belief on the part of many of the Mormon converts that Joseph Smith was a modern-day prophet and that his Book of Mormon was indeed the word of God. However, as one reads the detailed accounts of the crossing of the wilderness, one is impressed with another very important factor: the leadership of Brigham Young. Barely a month after arriving in the Salt Lake Valley, Young and his ever-faithful friend Spencer Kimball headed back to Winter Quarters to encourage others along the way to Salt Lake. They passed a caravan of more than 1500 already on the way. When he came to Winter Quarters, Young proposed to the twelve apostles a new hierarchy for the church with himself as the prophet, seer and revelator. He proposed himself, his nephew-in-law Spencer Kimball and his cousin Willard Richards to make up the First Presidency of the church. The twelve approved unanimously and with this action, the succession of the power of Joseph Smith rested fully on Brigham Young. In the following spring, May 1848, Young returned to Salt Lake with another group of immigrants. He never left Salt Lake again.

In December 1848, the Mormon High Council drew up a constitution for the

State of Deseret. Young was elected its first governor. Spencer Kimball was selected as chief justice of Deseret, despite the fact that he had no legal experience at all. For thirty years Brigham Young led "the Kingdom of God on the Earth" with an iron fist. He accepted no opposition. His rule was enforced by the strength of his personality and by physical intimidation of his enforcers, including the Danites. Opponents were sent away on long and difficult missionary trips or were excommunicated. Elections were held, but the ballots were not secret and the results were always a foregone conclusion.

Under Brigham's rule, with the help of influential leaders such as Orson and Parley Pratt and John Taylor (president after Young, shot in the jail in Carthage with Joseph Smith), Mormonism took a form significantly different from what had been practiced in Kirtland, Far West and Nauvoo. Joseph Smith was a spiritualist. Mormonism under his influence included prophecy, revelations, seer stones and miracles. Young was suspicious of these because his opponents could make use of them, too. In his entire career as a prophet and revelator he only published one rather mundane revelation. Rather, Young created a church relying more on submission to an earthly religious leadership, and whose manifestation of divine favor was material blessings. His church had more the flavor of Puritanism/Calvinism, with its work ethic, unadorned lifestyle, and sense of Manifest Destiny than the emotional and ecstatic flavor of modern Pentecostalism found in Smith's early movement.

Young himself became very wealthy. He was a successful farmer, rancher, factory builder and acquirer of water rights. All the evidence supports the conclusion that he was scrupulously honest in all his financial dealings. Those acquainted with modern Mormonism will see much of Brigham Young in the lives of the Saints today.

By 1851 there were sixteen branches and 11,354 Mormon immigrants in the Salt Lake area, growing wheat, corn, oats, millet, potatoes and more. Smith established settlements throughout Utah, sending settlers as far as Idaho, Arizona and Nevada. His followers founded the settlements of Las Vegas, Nevada and San Bernardino, California. By 1870, the Mormons had increased to 171 branches and 87,838 members. Much of the growth, of course, was from the very large families that were so strongly encouraged by Brigham Young, but immigrants from Europe continued in a steady flow to the Great Basin. During this period very few Americans were converted to the movement.

The Mormons attempted by all means possible, both legal and illegal, to minimize federal influence in Utah. In 1851, when President Zachary Taylor refused to back down in his efforts to exert control over the government of Deseret, Young said publicly, "But Zachary Taylor is dead and in hell, and I am glad of it." Taylor was very much alive when Young made this statement. He predicted that, "in the name of Jesus Christ, by the power of the Priesthood that's upon me...any President of the United States who lifts his finger against this people shall die an untimely death, and go to hell."[74]

Following the murder of Parley Pratt in May 1857, an expedition of anti-Mormon settlers from Arkansas passed through southern Utah. At the same time, there were rumors of federal troops entering Utah under orders from President Buchanan. In September 1857, in the isolated valley of Mountain Meadows, the sojourners were confronted by a group of Mormons, with John D. Lee at their head, as well as a group of Native Americans. The Gentiles held out in a tense standoff for four days, but finally surrendered to Lee. The prisoners were promised a safe escort to Cedar City. After marching them a short distance, the Mormons surrounded the settlers and massacred all the men and women and most of the children. A total of 120 were killed in the "Mountain Meadows Massacre."

Details of this tragedy are murky. After the massacre, Lee went directly to his close friend Brigham Young for advice. Young "wept like a child." He advised Lee that "not a drop of innocent blood has been shed." He told Lee that he would "sustain" all those who had taken part in the massacre, and asked him to "write a long letter laying all the blame on the Indians." To this day, most Mormons believe it was the Indians who were responsible for the massacre. This view is not supported by the evidence. Young later gave Lee three more wives and appointed him probate judge of Washington County.[75] John Lee was eventually convicted of the crime and executed.

We can assume that Young would not have ordered this massacre. He was too wise to provoke the federal response that would surely follow. However, he was complicit in the cover-up of a mass murder. In any event, partly as a result of this bloody affair, then-president James Buchanan decided to invade Utah. Thus ensued the Mormon War of 1857–58. The war did not amount to much. It was principally a political move on the part of Buchanan. Fifteen hundred federal troops approached Salt Lake City. Young mobilized the Nauvoo Legion, threatened to destroy the Federal army, and had the population retreat south, toward Provo. Troops entered the city briefly in June 1858, but the entire affair led to a standoff. Buchanan offered a general pardon to the "treasonous" Mormons.

## Mormon Teaching Under the Influence of Brigham Young

Brigham Young was not one given to claiming new doctrinal revelations. However, under his influence, Mormon teachings did develop in some significant ways. It will remain difficult to prove how many of the controversial teachings of Young were given to him by his mentor Joseph Smith and how many of them were the creations of Young himself. Probably most originated with Joseph Smith.

In a watershed event, Brigham Young published a letter in 1852 admitting that Mormons did in fact believe in and practice polygamy. He claimed that the practice had begun June 12, 1843, upon a revelation received by Smith. In 1878, a year after Brigham died, the Saints admitted openly that this was not true—that this was not when Smith began teaching polygamy. Under pressure from the mounting evidence, the church admitted "as early as 1831 the rightfulness of the plurality of wives under certain conditions was made known to Joseph Smith."[76] This admission came in the face of repeated, vehement, public declarations by Joseph Smith that he never supported or practiced the plurality of wives. Until 1852 the Mormons had consistently and unambiguously declared all charges of polygamy against their leaders were lies. John Taylor, President of the Mormon Church after Young, said in 1850, "We are accused here of polygamy and actions the most indelicate, obscene and disgusting, such that none but a corrupt and depraved heart could have contrived. These things are too outrageous to admit of belief."[77] Future Latter-day Saint President Taylor took his first plural wife in 1841, and had a total of ten by the time he gave this public denial. If Taylor's statements about polygamy are true (that it is obscene, disgusting and depraved), then they apply to his own polygamous situation.

We see here a clear pattern. Mormon leaders, most notably Joseph Smith and Brigham Young, did not for a moment hesitate to tell bold-faced lies to the "Gentiles." This was justified on the grounds that it was needed in order to protect the "Kingdom of God" from the ungodly Gentiles and to protect the faith and testimony of believers. More will be said on the deceitful "milk before meat" practice later. Such was the public leadership of Smith, Young and Taylor.

Also in 1852, Brigham preached that the biblical Adam was God and that Adam/God was a polygamist.

> "When our father Adam came into the Garden of Eden he came into it with a celestial body, and brought Eve, one of his wives, with him. He helped to make and organize this world. He is Michael, the Arch-angel, the Ancient of Days! About whom holy men have written and spoken—He is our Father and our God, and the only God with whom we have to do."[78]

Another doctrinal development of Brigham Young was to claim that God/Adam had sexual intercourse with Mary.

> That very babe that was cradled in the manger was begotten, not by Joseph, the husband of Mary, but by another Being. Do you inquire by whom? He was

> begotten by God our heavenly Father, by the process known to nature—just as men now create children.[79]

Young made this statement in a public address to a group that included the Speaker of the United States House of Representatives. Here he taught that God/Adam has a plurality of wives, which included Eve and Mary. Brigham taught that the Father and the Son appeared identical, except that God/Adam was older than the Son/Jesus.

In what could be perceived from a Christian perspective to be adding insult to injury, one of Young's closest advisers, Orson Pratt, added that Jesus was crucified, not for declaring that he was God in the flesh, but because he had a plurality of wives! These wives included Mary Magdalene, as well as Mary and Martha, the sisters of Lazarus.[80] Pratt's source for this historical information was not given at the time.

Why was Young so determined to push polygamy in the face of the world? It is difficult, of course, to nail down personal motivations, but one thought is that by committing the Saints to this course, he would dramatically reduce the rate of apostasy. A man who had plural wives had nowhere else to go but Utah. A plural wife also had few if any alternatives once she was brought into the system. It has been estimated that between ten and twenty percent of the households in Utah were polygamous at the height of the practice in the 1870s.[81]

Perhaps the most infamous teaching put forward by Brigham is known as the doctrine of blood atonement. The idea of this doctrine is that one's sins in this life could be "atoned for" by the shedding of that person's blood. We can see right away the moral and legal issues raised by enforcing this doctrine. Jedediah Grant, whose nickname was "Brigham's sledgehammer," said on this matter:

> I say that there are men and women that I would advise to go to the President immediately, and ask him to appoint a committee to attend to their case; and then let a place be selected, and let the committee shed their blood. We have those amongst us that are full of all manner of abominations, those who need to have their blood shed, for *water will not do*, their sins are too deep to dye."[82]

Brigham added:

> I have seen scores and hundreds of people for whom there would have been a chance (in the last resurrection there will be) if their lives had been taken and their blood spilled on the ground as a smoking incense to the Almighty, but

> who are now angels to the devil until our elder brother, Jesus Christ, uses them up—conquers death, hell and the grave. I have known a great many men who have left this church for whom there is no chance whatever for exaltation; but if their blood had been spilled it would have been better for them. The wickedness and ignorance of nations forbid this principle's being in full force, but the time will come when the law of God will be in full force.[83]

We can be grateful that this particular prophecy of Brigham Young has not yet been fulfilled. Note the use of the language from the Old Testament sacrificial system here. The thinly veiled threat of execution to those who would leave the Mormon group is chilling.

## Brigham Young Leaves the Stage

Controversy followed Brigham Young to the end. In 1871 he was arrested for "lewd and lascivious cohabitation" with sixteen of his wives. This was followed by his arrest in 1872 on several counts of murder for deaths that had occurred during the Mormon Wars. He was released on $200,000 bail—a massive sum at that time. The Mormon leadership counterattacked against the federal government by reconstituting the state of Deseret. A new constitution was drawn up. It was supported in an election without secret ballot by an overwhelming vote of 25,724 to 368. Young never went to trial. He largely removed himself from the public after these arrests but continued to rule Utah and the Saints from behind the scene until his death on August 28, 1877.

How are we to evaluate the life of Brigham Young and his part in forming the Latter-day Saint movement today? There is a sense in which his role is much less significant than that of Joseph Smith. No Mormon declares, "This is my testimony: Joseph Smith and Brigham Young are prophets and the Book of Mormon is the Word of God." The Mormon testimony stands or falls based on the character and ministry of Joseph Smith, not Brigham Young. However, as we will see in our chapter on modern-day Mormonism, the life and sayings of Brigham Young are nevertheless an integral part of what Mormons believe and how they view themselves. His additions to the *Doctrine and Covenants* of the church are considered the inspired Word of God. For the Latter-day Saints there is no Mormonism without Brigham Young.

In some significant ways, Young was a great man, especially as a leader of people. For us, however, it is his qualifications as a godly man and spiritual leader that are important. If we judge Young principally on these qualities, then his faults appear to greatly outweigh his leadership skills.

We are about to turn our attention to the scriptures of Mormonism, but one event that occurred just a few years after the death of Brigham Young bears mentioning now. On the death of Young, John Taylor succeeded to the presidency of the church. This is the man who was shot in the jail in Carthage, Illinois when Joseph and Hyrum were murdered. He was one of the strongest advocates of the plural marriage system and the father of thirty-five children. As long as the residents of Utah insisted on maintaining this system at any cost, there was no way for Utah to become a state in the Union. Hundreds of Mormon men were arrested and Taylor went into hiding. He died in 1887.

After a two-year vacancy, John Taylor was succeeded in the presidency by Wilford Woodruff. Soon after taking the role, Woodruff issued a manifesto (September 1890). In the pronouncement, he declared that celestial marriage was the ideal for the Kingdom of God, but he officially suspended the practice in the Utah church in order to prevent the destruction of the church. Woodruff did not end his own plural marriages. He lived with his wives until his death and was convicted of polygamy. However, new plural marriage ceremonies were ended. And so, on January 4, 1896, Utah was admitted to the Union as the forty-fifth state.

# Chapter 6

# The Book of Mormon

"This is my testimony: Joseph Smith is a prophet and the Book of Mormon is the Word of God." We have already investigated the first half of this testimony and found it wanting. We will now proceed to analyze the second half of this testimony, "The Book of Mormon is the Word of God." Joseph Smith called the Book of Mormon "the most correct of any book on earth and the keystone of our religion."[84] We will look carefully at the quality of this keystone of the Mormon faith.

We have already considered the history of the Book of Mormon. Joseph Smith claimed to have written it by miraculous translation from "Reformed Egyptian" on golden plates. For this purpose he used at some times a seer stone, at other times the "Urim and Thummim," stones found with the golden plates and hidden in the Hill of Cumorah.

The following is a brief summary of the contents of the *Book of Mormon: Another Testament of Jesus Christ*. It is adapted from the work of a good friend, Joe Fields.[85] With his permission, I have adapted the original summary.

## Introduction

The Book of Mormon claims to be the record of God's dealings with the inhabitants of ancient Mesoamerica (approx. 2000 BC to AD 421). The record tracks the history of two civilizations. The first nation, known as the Jaredites, is claimed to have come by boat to the Americas (Isthmus of Tehuantepec/Southern Mexico/Guatemala) when God confounded the tongues at the Tower of Babel (Genesis 11:5–9). After more than a thousand years, the entire nation is destroyed by the Lamanites, the alleged ancestors of the American Indians (Book of Ether).

The second nation is claimed to have come from Jerusalem during the first year of King Zedekiah (597 BC). Rebellion soon divided the nation into two factions, the Nephites and the Lamanites. Throughout the book the Nephites are preaching the story of Jesus, calling unbelievers to be "born again" just after 100 BC (Mosiah 27:25), and making "Christians" as early as 73 BC (Alma 46:15).

This history is recorded on sheets of metal and plates of brass. On or about the year AD 421, the last Nephite prophet, Moroni, sealed up the record and hid it on the Hill Cumorah, near to present-day Palmyra, New York. On September 21, 1823, the resurrected Moroni visited Joseph Smith and revealed to Joseph the location of the plates and the two stones that were used for interpreting the plates. The Book of Mormon was first published in 1830.

## First Book of Nephi: 600–570 BC

Lehi, his wife Sariah and their four sons, Laman, Lemuel, Sam and Nephi are called to flee from the destruction of Jerusalem during the reign of Zedekiah (2 Kings 24:18). For eight years they wander in a wilderness near the Red Sea, being led by a ball (1 Nephi 16:16). During this time any who waver in unbelief are turned to dark-skinned people (12:23). The corruption of the Bible is foretold (13:26–27) and the establishment of "other books" that must be followed in order to be saved is predicted (13:39–40). It is prophesied that the gospel will be lost, but will be returned after many generations to a remnant of the Lamanites (Indians), presumably by Joseph Smith (15:13). Coming to a great "sea," it is divinely revealed that they will build a ship (17:8). In this ship, they will be taken to the "promise land (sic)" (18:8). Utilizing a compass (18:12,21) which only Nephi knows how to manage, they arrive at the "promise land" (18:23–25). There they find cows, oxen, horses and donkeys—none of which lived in the New World at that time (18:25). Nephi makes plates of ore recording the events of those who have come "out of the waters of baptism" (20:1). He closes with prophecies regarding the future destinies of his people and of the human race.

## Second Book of Nephi: 588–545 BC

Lehi proclaims, "Jerusalem is destroyed," and the Americas are the new "land of promise." Explanation is given for the origin of the devil (2:17) and the fall of man. We learn that it is a good thing that Adam fell (2:23-25). Lehi claims to be "a descendant of Joseph who was carried captive into Egypt" (3:4). He prophesies the coming of Joseph Smith, the seer "great like unto Moses" (3:7–9). Lehi dies, Nephi takes leadership of the nation and divides from Laman. The Nephites build a temple like the temple of

Solomon. The Lamanites, who are white people, are cursed at that time with a "skin of blackness" (5:14–21). The also learn the use of iron and steel over 2000 years before they were first used in the Americas (5:15). The history of Israel is reviewed with an emphasis on "covenants" with "all" the house of Israel gathering in "all their lands of promise" (9:2).

The complete plan of salvation is revealed by Lehi in 545 BC. The Americas are claimed as a "better land" of promise (10:20). The book of Isaiah ch. 2–14 is quoted, often word for word, from the King James Version (ch. 12–24). The destruction of Judah, Jerusalem, Assyria and Babylon is declared. The coming of Christ to America after the resurrection is promised (26:1–3). In a clear anachronism, Synagogues are described as existing in the 6th century BC (26:26). The Book of Mormon will reveal things from the beginning of the world to the end. It will be delivered to one man and witnessed by three (27:7–12). Many will reject the book saying, "A Bible! A Bible! We have got a Bible, and there cannot be any more Bible" (29:3–10). Another book is forthcoming from the "lost tribes of Israel" (29:13). The book closes with a review of the complete plan of salvation, hundreds of years before it was revealed in the New Testament (30–33).

## Book of Jacob: 545–421 BC

Jacob is commissioned to write about the history of the Nephites. He preaches against pride, materialism, and plural marriages. Plural marriages are an abomination (2:12–28). The Lamanites are now acknowledged as being more faithful than the Nephites. A warning is given that if the Nephites do not repent, the Lamanites' "skins will be whiter than yours" (3:8). The atonement of Christ is preached as something to accept now (544 BC), even though it is recognized that Christ has not yet been born (4:11–13). A religious teacher named Sherem confronts Jacob, telling him that he should not be preaching Christ but should be helping people to obey the Law of Moses. Sherem claims he would not deny Christ but he desires a sign from the Holy Spirit to believe. God smites Sherem to the ground, he confesses Christ, calls his followers to deny what he has taught them, and dies (7:1–20). The Nephites attempt to restore the Lamanites.

## Book of Enos: 544–421 BC

The book of Enos has only twenty-seven verses. Before Nephi dies he ordains Enos and gives him the plates. Most of what he records is about the struggle between the Nephites and the Lamanites. Again, we meet cows and horses in the New World—2000 years before they were introduced there (v. 21) which is an indisputable fact. He passes the plates on to his son Jarom.

## Book of Jarom: 420–399 BC

The book of Jarom has only fifteen verses. Jarom begins by acknowledging that the writers before him have revealed the true plan of salvation (1:2). The Nephites are using iron and steel—2000 years before they were seen in the New World (v. 8). They are to observe the Law of Moses and to look forward to the coming of the Messiah as though it has already happened (v. 11). Jarom passes the plates on to his son Omni.

## Book of Omni: 361–130 BC

The book of Omni has only thirty verses. Omni writes the first three verses and then conferred the task of writing to his son Amaron who writes the next five verses. No matter how wicked the Nephites have become, God will fulfill his promises (v. 5–6). Chemish writes verse 9. Abinadom writes verses 10–11, concluding with the words written by Amaleki. They discover a people from the land of Zarahemla. This nation had also come from Jerusalem during the reign of Zedekiah (v. 14-15). Upon arrival the people of Zarahemla had encountered a nation from one called Coriantumr whose parents had come to America from the tower of Babel (v. 22). The Nephites preach the redemption of Jesus (v. 26). The plates are passed on to King Benjamin the son of Mosiah (v. 23-25).

## Words of Mormon: 385 AD

Containing only eighteen verses, the events of this book are reported to have occurred many years after the coming of Christ. Mormon delivers the records over to Moroni. His writings are an abridgment in the history from Jacob to the reign of King Benjamin (v. 3).

Thousands of Lamanites have been slain but King Benjamin has been able to bring peace to the land (v. 14–18).

## Book of Mosiah: 130–92 BC

King Benjamin hands down to Mosiah, his son, the plates of brass, the plates of Nephi, the sword of Laban, and the ball which led them through the wilderness (1:16). They meet at the temple for a time of great sacrifice and burnt offerings according to the Law of Moses (2:3). Because of the multitude gathered there, no one could hear King Benjamin. Therefore his lesson is recorded for all to read (2:8). Mosiah is appointed their king. The atonement of Christ and remission of sins is proclaimed (3:1–5:30). Jesus is called the Father (3:8). All those accepting his words are called "children of Christ"

(5:7, 124 BC). Priests are appointed from among the Nephites (6:3). Ammon recounts the history of the Limhi people, with the discovery of gold plates, ruins of buildings, artifacts, and weapons (8:8–11). The definition of a seer is given (8:16–17). The record of Zeniff from the search of Zarahemla to deliverance from the Lamanites is revealed (ch. 9–22). Noah is condemned for polygamy (whereas he is praised for polygamy in the Book of Abraham) (11:2). Noah is said to have built many spacious buildings, an enormous palace, a temple and a tower, which could view other lands (11:8–12). The prophet Abinadi condemns the priest of Noah's time for failing to live by the Law of Moses (even though it had not yet been established at Sinai) (12:33). 1 Corinthians 15 is quoted—150 years before it was written (16:6-10). Atonement is foreshadowed in the Law of Moses (16:14). Abinadi further observes that the message of Jesus' atonement is not yet binding on mankind (13:27–28). Alma begins to preach Jesus, to baptize in the name of Jesus and people receive the gift of the Holy Spirit (18:10). He baptizes 204 converts and establishes the "church of Christ," the "kingdom of God," and teaches them to observe the Sabbath day (18:15–23). Alma rejects their offer of kingship and becomes their high priest (23:16). Seven churches are established in Zarahemla by Alma (25:23). Many fall away and begin to persecute the church (ch. 26–28). Mosiah interprets the plates of gold using the two stones fastened into two rims (28:11–13). The role of a king is rejected and judges are set up to lead the nation. Alma becomes the first chief judge and high priest (29:42).

## Book of Alma: 96–53 BC

Alma is the longest of all of the books, containing sixty-three chapters. It is the most varied in its content, with doctrine, history, prophecy and revelation. The Nephites have silk in the New World—1500 years before it was brought by the Europeans (1:29). Nehor battles against a false religion called priestcraft that holds that all mankind will be saved (ch. 1-2). The Nephites battle against the Amlicite unbelievers who are distinguished by "marking themselves with red in their foreheads" (3:2). Three thousand five hundred souls are baptized into the church in 86–85 BC (4:4–5). Alma appoints Nephihah as chief judge but maintains the office of high priest (4:17). Alma calls his generation and all generations to repent and be born again in 83 BC (5:48–50). He calls men to be washed by the blood of the lamb, going into baptism (7:14-15). Warning is given to the Nephites not to forsake the Lord. Lehi is identified as a descendant of Manasseh (Alma 10:3). Nephite coinage is identified and explained—despite the fact that there is no evidence of coinage in the New World before Columbus (ch. 11). Zeezrom and Amulek debate the existence of God (11:21–35) and the *Trinity*

(11:44). Alma preaches to Antionah the plan of redemption from the foundations of the world in 82 BC (12:19–33). Qualifications for the high priesthood of Christians are given (ch. 13). Alma and Amulek are cast into prison, then an earthquake sets them free (14:17–27).

Alma teaches that after his resurrection Jesus will appear to the Nephites (16:20). The conversion of Lamoni to the plan of salvation in 90 BC is described (19:13). The conversion of the whole household of Lamoni's father is related (22:23). Zarahemla is identified as the place of their first landing (22:30). We are told of the conversion of the Lamanites *en masse* to become the nation of Anti-Nephi-Lehies and to no longer have the dark skin "curse" (23:17-18, 2 Nephi 5:21). Warnings are given against "falling away" after being enlightened by the Spirit (24:30). The Law of Moses was not fulfilled yet; it must be kept, looking forward to Christ (25:15). The decrees of God are unalterable (29:4). Korihor, the antichrist, teaches that death is the end of man (30:6–18). The Zoramite view of election and their claim as the chosen people is presented (31:16–18).

Infinite atonement is illustrated in Moses as a type, foreshadowing the atonement of Christ (33:19–34:31). The mysteries of atonement are not yet fully known (37:11). The word of Christ is compared to the ball or compass that led their way in the wilderness (37:38–44). People have received the gift of the "Holy Ghost" one hundred years before Pentecost (39:6). Alma justifies the teaching of atonement as necessary to the plan of redemption in 73 BC (39:15–19). The state of the soul between death and the resurrection is discussed (40:11). The first resurrection is defined (40:15-20). The scheme of redemption is given (ch. 42). A prediction of the falling away and destruction of the Nephites is made (45:10–11). Alma is taken up and his body buried by God (45:18–19). People are called Christians in 73 BC (46:13–16). The last sixteen chapters deal mainly with the history of battles with the Nephites. Dozens of large cities are built and destroyed. Huge populations grow and are destroyed in great wars, none of which is supported by any archaeological find to date.

## Book of Helaman: 52–2 BC

This book contains the account of the conversion of tens of thousands of Lamanites (ch. 3). Many buildings and cities are built of cement in 49 BC—1500 years before cement was first used in the Americas (3:9–11). The church of the Nephites begins to dwindle in unbelief (4:23). The Holy Spirit appears in a pillar of fire and 300 are filled with fire to "speak forth marvelous words" (5:43-49). A nation called the Gadianton begins an order of "secret signs, secret words, secret oaths and covenants." Such secret oaths and covenants are condemned (6:22–25) (which seems inconsistent with Smith's later incorporation of secret oaths and covenants in temple ritual). The coming of the

Messiah is compared to the brazen serpent of Moses (Numbers 21:1–9, Helaman 8:14). The five messengers find the chief judge dead following the prophecy of Nephi (ch. 9). Nephi is given the power to smite the land with famine and pestilence (10:6). People are part of "the church" before Jesus is born (11:21). A prophet named Samuel foretells that Christ will be born in five years and that the night before will be as light as day: "no darkness" (14:2–5). Another sign will come at the death of Christ. The sign will be three days of darkness (14:17–20). Unbelievers find this unreasonable to accept and reject the coming of Christ (16:18).

## Book of Third Nephi: 1 BC–35 AD

The Messiah is born, the sun sets, but the night is as bright as day. A star appears. It can be clearly seen by all and many unbelievers are converted (ch. 1). The Lamanites who are converted have the dark skin curse removed and become white like the Nephites (2:14–16). Battles continue with the secret order of the Gadiantons. At the time of the death of Jesus darkness covers the land for three days, cities sink into the sea, and the whole face of the land becomes deformed (8:1–23). The land remains dark until the resurrection of Jesus when he appears to thousands (ch.9-10). Baptism by immersion is clarified (11:26). Jesus commissions twelve others and repeats the Sermon on the Mount for the Nephites (ch.1–14). Jesus promises to visit other lands and other people to gather them in from the four quarters of the earth (ch. 16). He tells them that he will establish a New Jerusalem in North America (20:22) and that a prophet "like Moses" will come to them (presumably this is a reference to Joseph Smith). If they do not listen to this prophet, they will be cut off (20:23). Jesus heals the people and teaches them many things. Three witnesses/apostles are promised that they will never die and that they will be sinless (28:36–40).

## Book of Fourth Nephi: 36–321 AD

Not long after Jesus preached to them, the entire Nephite and Lamanite population is converted to Christ, ushering in a period of great harmony, peace and wealth (1:2 f). As a result, the Nephites become very white (1:10). However, after two centuries the church falls into many evil practices.

## Book of Mormon: 322–421 AD

The three Nephite witnesses are taken away because of the unbelief of the people. Mormon, a mighty general, commands forty-two thousand men against the

Lamanites in a dreadful battle. The Lamanites become darker and filthier than they have ever been before because of their sin (5:15). They take the land (South America) and the Nephites are left with the land of Cumorah (North America, 6:4). Knowing they will be destroyed, Mormon hides the plates on the hill Cumorah (presumably near Palmyra, New York) (6:6). A massive battle, resulting in the death of 230,000 men, occurs at the Hill Cumorah. Native Americans are reminded that they are direct descendants of the Jews (7:2). Mormon is foretold that the plates will be discovered during a time of great religious controversy in the land (ch. 8). Those who will find the plates are told that the words on the plates of Nephi are without fault and that those who demand to see the plates will be killed (8:17–18). He proclaims the permanence of miraculous gifts as long as belief is present (9:15–25). He ends by challenging others not to be critical of his imperfect records because of his limited familiarity with "Reformed Egyptian" (9:31–32).

## Book of Ether: (about 2000 BC)

Moroni writes the book of Ether as an account of the Jaredites who escaped from the Tower of Babel (1:33). They are promised to be a greater nation than any other (1:43). They follow a cloud through a wilderness to the sea. They are told that the place they are going (the Americas) is not yet inhabited—a fairly obvious error (2:5). Building eight vessels by God's design, they prepare to cross the sea. The vessels are cubic in shape. Jared becomes concerned that God's design is not a very good one in that if these vessels are airtight, they will suffocate and there will be no light. For this reason he informs the Lord that they need to breathe or they will die (2:17–20). God allows them to put a hole in the top and in the bottom of the boat that they can open or seal at any time. Concerned about the darkness, Jared petitions God to touch sixteen stones that will be used as windows in the barges. Miraculously Jared beholds the "flesh and blood" finger of Jesus turning the stones clear. Later two of these stones are sealed up with the plates that will be discovered by Joseph Smith (3:1–9, 3:23–24, 6:2). Their journey across the ocean takes 344 days (6:11). The Jaredites possess iron technology (7:9), as well as silk, cattle, horses, elephants—none of these existed in the Americas at the time—as well as "cureloms and cumoms" (9:17–19). Not long after their landing, the Jaredites become consumed in civil strife. Although they number about two million mighty men, after war and carnage all are killed but one. Moroni claims to see Jesus face-to-face. Whereupon he is given the message of the future coming of the "New Jerusalem" in the New World (13:3). The lone survivor of this generation is Coriantumr, who will later be discovered by the Nephites (15:32).

## Book of Moroni: 400–AD 421

Moroni writes to teach the Lamanites how to ordain priests and teachers and how to administer the law (ch. 1-7). He condemns infant baptism and original sin (8:5–8). Moroni seals up the record in AD 421, promising that any reader who is sincere can ask God and he will be shown that these things are true (10:2–4). Moroni makes it clear that miraculous gifts, including speaking in tongues, will not cease (10:19).

## An Analysis of the Book of Mormon

With our summary completed, we proceed to an analysis of the Book of Mormon. How is a reasonable person to view the "golden book?" Is it, as Mormons everywhere testify, "the Word of God?" Is the Book of Mormon, as Joseph Smith claimed, "the most correct of any book on earth?" A fair analysis will reach a negative conclusion on these questions.

One thing we can say with confidence is that this story is fiction. As a historical proposition, the story of the Jaredites, Lamanites and Nephites is unsustainable. No serious student of history and archaeology has reached any other conclusion. With dozens of massive cities, many built of concrete; with battles in which many millions were killed; with at least two centuries during which Christianity was the principal religion throughout Mesoamerica; with large numbers of horses, cattle, donkeys, pigs, camels and elephants, as well as coinage; with wheat and barley, rather than the native maize and potatoes as crops, it stretches credulity beyond reason to believe that there would be absolutely no physical record of these things anywhere in Central America.

The fact remains, however, that this is the case. There is no supporting evidence for any of the unique claims of the Book of Mormon with regard to the history of the New World. All the evidence from Mesoamerica in the first three centuries AD points to a form of religion with no affinity to Christianity—at a time the Book of Mormon claims it was the only religion practiced there. None of the cities named in the Book of Mormon have been found. No evidence of coinage, horses, pigs, wheat, elephants, donkeys or any of the other anachronistic objects indicated in the Book of Mormon has been found. At this point, to hold out for the possibility that such evidence will emerge is not rational. The question of the historical reliability of the Book of Mormon is a settled matter. It is pure fiction.

We can agree with Mormon author Ross T. Christensen of Brigham Young University when he speaks of the Book of Mormon: "If the book's history is fallacious, its doctrine cannot be genuine."[86] The history is fallacious. The statements of the Smithsonian Institute and the National Geographic Society represent the unanimous verdict of (non-Mormon) archaeologists:

> "The Smithsonian Institution has never used the Book of Mormon in any way as a scientific guide. Smithsonian archaeologists see no connection between the archaeology of the New World and the subject matter of the Book."[87]

> "With regard to the cities mentioned in the Book of Mormon, neither representatives of the National Geographic Society nor archeologists connected with any other institution of equal prestige have ever used the Book of Mormon in locating historic ruins in middle America or elsewhere.[88]

If the Hill Cumorah of the Book of Mormon is the place where Joseph Smith found the plates of Nephi in upstate New York, where is the evidence of a great battle which killed 230,000 men at this site? If, as Mormons claim, the location of the events of the Book of Mormon is Central America, how did the plates end up in upstate New York? Did Nephi travel 4000 miles to leave them in a place convenient for Joseph Smith to find them? If the Hill Cumorah of found in the Book of Mormon is actually an unidentified site somewhere in Central America, then how did the plates of Nephi get to upstate New York, and how did it come to be that two different hills came to have the same name? These questions are literally impossible to answer in a way which is reasonable.

The claim of the Book of Mormon that native tribes in Central America are the direct lineal descendants of Jewish immigrants is insupportable. It is an established fact, based on DNA analysis, that Native Americans, both in North and South America, are descended from East Asians, not from Semites. When Mormon molecular biologist Simon G. Southerton published his findings to this effect in *Losing a Lost Tribe: Native Americans, DNA and the Mormon Church*, he was threatened with excommunication by the Utah church and ultimately left the Saints. Joseph Smith could safely make these speculative assumptions in his time, but modern science has revealed his folly.

Moving on from historical and archaeological problems, the Book of Mormon has a number of other defects that show it is not "the most perfect book ever written," and is not the inspired Word of God. We should remember that not only do Mormons claim that the inscription on the golden plates was inspired, but that Joseph Smith's "translation" from these plates was also inspired. A major difficulty for this claim is the fact that the original edition, published in 1830 by Joseph Smith, had thousands of elementary spelling and grammatical errors. These errors are in a translation from the "Reformed Egyptian" which was supposedly inspired by God. The number and types of errors in the original are so embarrassing that the Mormon Church has tried to suppress this first edition. Even current editions of the Book of Mormon include some rather blatantly bad grammar. For example, in 2 Nephi 24:23, we find the dubious English word *besom*. In 2 Nephi 24:23 we find the word disannul. 2 Nephi 24:27 has the sentence, *I was an hungered, for I had fasted...* Alma 8:26 has the grammatically questionable *and did molten out of a rock sixteen small stones...* Ether 3:1 has *unwearyingness*—a word of dubious derivation.

Significantly, by 1842 all but two of the eleven "witnesses" to the original Book of Mormon and the golden plates had either apostatized from Joseph's movement or had died. In hopes of putting behind him the poorly written original manuscript, with its thousands of grammatical and spelling errors, Smith had it buried under the Nauvoo House, saying at the event, "I have had trouble enough with this thing."[89]

Literary analysis of the Book of Mormon leads to the conclusion that the writing style of the book is not of a high quality. One finds in the book the phrase "And it came to pass" hundreds of times. The style is sufficiently repetitive that literary critic Mark Twain famously described the book as "chloroform in print."[90] It is difficult to explain how the plates of Nephi came to have Greek words on them, such as Alpha and Omega (3 Nephi 9:18) and the Greek name Timothy (3 Nephi 19:4).

Joseph Smith claimed, as Mormons still do today, that the Book of Mormon contains the "fullness of the gospel." It is interesting, then, that the book of Mormon contains only a relatively small proportion of the [biblically deviant] teachings that are unique to the Latter-day Saints. Below are a few of the important Mormon teachings which are not found anywhere in the Book of Mormon:

- God is the product of eternal progression.
- There is a plurality of gods.
- Men may become gods.
- The trinity is three separate gods.
- There is no eternal punishment.
- The pre-existence of souls (humans exist as disembodied souls before their physical birth).
- There are three degrees of glory in the afterlife: the celestial, the terrestrial and the telestial.
- We have a Mother in heaven.
- There are numerous details of temple worship and ceremonies.
- God authorizes celestial marriage (marriage for eternity).
- There is a post-resurrection Melchizedek Priesthood and an Aaronic Priesthood.
- People may be baptized for the dead.

- God the Father has a physical body.

Some of these deviant ideas have already been discussed. Others will be covered in the chapter on the *Doctrine and Covenants* and *The Pearl of Great Price*, where most of these teachings are published. It is interesting that the "fullness of the gospel" in the Book of Mormon was free of these (false) doctrines of Mormonism. We can assume this is because in 1830 Joseph Smith had not yet conceived of these doctrines.

The Book of Mormon contains not only abundant false doctrines but also numerous factual errors (assuming that the Bible is reliable). Alma says about Melchizedek that he "reigned under his father" (Alma 13:18). This contradicts Hebrews 7:3. In the Book of Mormon we are told that it is good that Adam sinned (2 Nephi 2:23–25), because his fall is the reason that humans exist on the earth. There are many obviously contrived "prophecies" of the Messiah in the Book of Mormon. For example, in Mosiah 3:5–7 there is a prediction (about 120 BC) that the Messiah's name will be Jesus Christ, that his mother will have the name Mary, that blood will come from his pores,[91] and that he will be crucified. Anyone can see that here Smith is taking later biblical information and reading it back into bogus "prophecy".

We could continue for many pages listing the historical and doctrinal errors of the Book of Mormon. The most obvious error from a biblical perspective is its confusion of the Mosaic and the Christian covenants. This goes beyond confusion, because the New Testament writers clearly state that the Gospel was kept as a biblical "mystery," only to be revealed by Jesus and his apostles. We have a number of scriptures that express this truth:

Concerning the Gospel, Paul said to the Colossians:

> The *mystery* has been kept hidden for ages and generations, but is now disclosed to the saints. To them [the saints Paul is speaking to] God has chosen to make known among the Gentiles the glorious riches of this mystery, which is Christ in you, the hope of glory (Colossians1:26–27 emphasis added).

To the Ephesians he said, concerning the gospel message:

> And he made known to us the *mystery* of his will according to his good pleasure, which he purposed in Christ, to be put into effect when the times will have reached their fulfillment—to bring all things in heaven and on earth together under one head, even Christ (Ephesians 1:9–10 emphasis added).

Paul is even more specific about the fact that the mystery was not revealed before the time of Christ:

> Surely you have heard about the administration of God's grace that was given to me for you, that is, the *mystery* made known to me by revelation, as I have already written briefly. In reading this, then, you will be able to understand my insight into the mystery of Christ, which was not made known to men in other generation as it has now been revealed by the Spirit to God's holy apostles and prophets (Ephesians 3:2–5 emphasis added).

Paul was given the mission to spread the Gospel to the Gentiles—to share about his grace:

> ...and to make plain to everyone the administration of this *mystery* which for ages past was kept hidden in God, who created all things (Ephesians 3:9 emphasis added).

Paul makes it clear that the gospel was not revealed in prophetic Scripture before the time of Christ:

> Now to Him who has power to strengthen you according to my gospel and the proclamation of Jesus Christ according to the revelation of the sacred secret kept silent for long ages, but now revealed and made known through the prophetic Scriptures... (Romans 16:25–26, HCSB).

From these and other passages in the New Testament it is clear that the gospel message was withheld or veiled from mankind until the coming of Christ and the sending forth of his witnesses to spread the news of salvation by the blood of Jesus. This biblical teaching is in unambiguous contradiction with statements in the Book of Mormon. We have seen a large number of examples in the summary of the Book of Mormon above. For example, in 2 Nephi 31:17 we find a comprehensive New Testament "plan of salvation." "For the gate by which ye should enter is repentance and baptism by water; and then cometh a remission of your sins by fire and by the Holy Ghost." Earlier we are told by Nephi to be baptized "in the name of my Beloved Son" (2 Nephi 31:12). This command is being given, according to Joseph Smith, in 545 BC. We can appreciate Smith's zeal to support the biblical teaching that baptism is necessary for salvation (Acts 2:38, 22:16), but it is an obvious error to put the command into the mouth of a "Lamanite" almost 600 years before the "mystery which was kept hidden" was brought to light by God.

Consider a few more examples of doctrinal anachronism in the Book of Mormon. The atonement of Christ is preached in 421 BC in Jacob 4:11-13. Nephites are called "children of Christ" (Mosiah 5:7) and are forgiven by the atoning blood of Jesus (Mosiah 4:2) in about 124 BC. Native Central Americans are "baptized in the name of the Lord (Mosiah 18:10), the Holy Spirit is received (Mosiah 18:12-13), and the "church of Christ" is established (Mosiah 18:17) by Alma—all before 100 BC. Later, about 83 BC, Alma calls the Nephites to be born again (Alma 5:48-50) and to be washed by the blood of the lamb in baptism (Alma 7:14-15). A great number of examples in the Book of Mormon could be added to these.

Making things even more confusing, the Book of Mormon has people applying the Old Covenant system of sacrifices and teaching the necessity of following the Law of Moses *after* they had already received the message of forgiveness by the blood of Jesus. In the book of Galatians, Paul makes it clear that those who are in Christ are not required to observe the laws in the Old Covenant (Galatians 2:15–21, 4:8–11, 21–31; also Acts 15:1–29). Right after baptizing 204 into Christ, Alma teaches them to observe the Sabbath (Mosiah 18:15–13). The Nephites are commanded in 399 BC to "keep the law of Moses and the Sabbath" (Jarom 1:5), and prophets and priests teach the law of Moses (Jarom 1:11), long after the same Nephites had accepted the atonement of Christ. In 2 Nephi 25:24–27 people are baptized into Christ, made alive in Christ, yet still commanded to keep the Law of Moses (545 BC). You can find no equivalent teachings or practices in the New Testament.

Add to this an apparent lack of knowledge of actual Jewish practices in the Book of Mormon. In Alma 30:3 we are told that, despite already having been baptized into Christ, the Nephites "were strict in observing the ordinances of God according to the Law of Moses." Yet in the Book of Mormon, there is no evidence of the Day of Atonement, the Passover, any of the dietary laws, burnt offerings, grain offerings, guilt offerings—indeed there is virtually no evidence whatsoever of knowledge of the actual laws of Moses in the Book of Mormon. This inconsistency is difficult to explain. In the chapter on reaching out to Mormons we will provide a study on the confusion of covenants that can be used in sharing with our Latter-day Saint friends.

A prophecy is given in 1 Nephi 13:26–27, supposedly in about 570 BC, that after the time of the twelve apostles a "great and abominable church which is most abominable above all other churches" will arise and that this church will "have taken away from the gospel of the Lamb many parts which are plain and most precious; and also many covenants of the Lord have they taken away. And all this have they done that they might pervert the right ways of the Lord, that they might blind the eyes and harden the hearts of the children of men." It is clear, as we process the teachings of Joseph Smith, that he is "prophesying" the Roman Catholic Church. He is also "prophesying" that the Roman Church changed the Bible to suit its purposes, by deleting parts it did not like. What are the "plain and most precious" parts of the New Testament that the church removed? We aren't told specifically, but we can assume that they include some of the teachings that were revealed by Joseph Smith in his Book of Mormon and later in the *Doctrine and Covenants.*

This begs the question: Has this prophecy been fulfilled? Is the claim sustainable that an evil and abominable church removed entire sections of the Scripture? Anyone acquainted with the history of the New Testament text can answer this question. The claim is patently false. Several New Testament manuscripts have survived from the second century, as well as entire New Testaments from the fourth century, not to mention tens of thousands of quotes from all the New Testament books in the writings of the church fathers in the first three centuries. It is impossible to sustain the claim that a fallen church removed plain and precious teachings from the New Testament. The Church certainly could not have removed "plain and precious promises" from the Hebrew Old Testament, as we have the Dead Sea Scrolls which date from several decades before the Church began in approximately 30 AD. Besides, the Jews certainly would not have allowed the Christian Church to remove parts of the Hebrew Bible. This "prophecy" was inserted by Smith to justify his own unbiblical teachings. This fiction was made up by Jospeh Smith 2400 years after the alleged removal of the "plain and precious promises" from the Old Testament events. Moreover, the evidence for the history of the Greek New Testament shows it to be clearly untrue.[92]

## Conclusion

In this brief analysis, we have not even discussed whether it is believable that Joseph Smith actually dug up golden plates at the Hill Cumorah and that he translated them from the "Reformed Egyptian" on the plates. Given the evidence, it is reasonable to conclude that there are no such plates and there never were.

We now ask, is the Book of Mormon the Word of God, as our Mormon friends testify, and "the most correct of any book on earth?" Further, is it "Another Testament of Jesus Christ?" No matter how much faith is claimed for inspiration, these claims cannot be sustained in view of the evidence from the text itself. The Book of Mormon cannot be substantiated as the revealed word of God. It is not another testament of Jesus Christ.

# Chapter 7

# Mormon Teaching: Doctrine and Covenants and The Pearl of Great Price

A fair analysis of the Church of Jesus Christ of Latter-day Saints will include a discussion of the central claims of the religion. It has already been stated that the majority of the doctrines which are unique to Mormonism are not found in the Book of Mormon. We have speculated that this is because Smith had not conceived of many of these doctrines when he wrote the Book of Mormon in 1828–29. Most important Mormon theology, doctrine, and practices unique to the group are found in the *Doctrine and Covenants* and *The Pearl of Great Price*.

The majority of this chapter is given to a description and analysis of the content of these two books. It should be noted that not all important teachings and practices of the Mormon Church are found in *Doctrine and Covenants* (henceforth *D&C*) and *The Pearl of Great Price*. Joseph Smith, Brigham Young and others gave additional teaching to the Mormon movement that have become part of the Latter-day Saint faith, yet is not found in any of its important scriptures. Therefore we will be examining such additional documents as *Teachings of the Church*, *Teachings of the Prophet Joseph Smith*, *Journal of Discourses*, the sermons of Joseph Smith, and the writings of Brigham Young to round out our picture of what is believed and taught by the Latter-day Saints.

## Doctrine and Covenants

The text now known as *Doctrine and Covenants* was first published in 1833 in Kirtland under the title *A Book of Commandments for the Government of the Church of Christ*.

Two years later, an expanded version was published at Kirtland with the current title. Later editions added new "revelations" of Joseph Smith up until his death in 1844. In 1847, one additional section was added by Brigham Young, as well as a Manifesto concerning polygamy in 1890 and a new "revelation" allowing the priesthood to blacks in 1978. There are 138 sections plus two "official declarations" in *Doctrine and Covenants.*

The main content of the sections of *D&C* is "revelations" given to Smith in response to particular situations. In this sense, the material is similar to the Muslim *Qur'an,* which is essentially a series of "revelations" to Muhammad to deal with particular issues as they came up. For this reason, both *D&C* and the *Qur'an* are repetitive and are often described by non-practitioners as rather boring. Nearly all the sections are written as if they are revelations to Joseph. In other words, Smith represents them as being channeled through him—that it is not he himself who is speaking. The revelations purport to be variously the words of the Father, Jesus Christ, Nephi, or John the Baptist. We will see that near the end of the sections of *D&C,* Joseph Smith begins to speak in first person. It appears that by the time he reached Nauvoo, Smith felt confident enough in his own authority to give direct revelation, rather than creating the impression that he was simply the instrument through which the revelations were given.
Another feature of *D&C* to bear in mind is that the earlier letters, like the Book of Mormon, have relatively little of what we would describe as heretical teaching. We see a turning point in about 1832 when Smith began to produce revelations which entail the bizarre theology and controversial teachings the Christian world generally associates with Mormonism.

We will not consider the content of all 138 sections, but will instead pull out representative texts, focusing on a small number of the sections that are of greater importance to understanding Mormon beliefs.

## Summary of *Doctrine and Covenants*

Fittingly, in Section 1 of *D&C* is a pronouncement from God that Joseph Smith, will receive commandments from heaven (1:17). The sections that follow (2–138) are in mostly chronological order, with some notable exceptions.

In 3:20 we learn that the Lamanites (Native Americans) will be saved. In these early sections there are hundreds of quotations from both the Old and the New Testament, written as if they were part of a new revelation from God. For example, in 4:4–7 we read "for behold the field is white already to harvest," and "faith, hope, charity and love...," "Ask and ye shall receive; knock and it shall be opened unto you." The phrase "the field is white already to harvest" is found dozens of times in *Doctrine and Covenants.*

In 5:3 is the command to Joseph, "Do not show the plates to anyone unless I tell you." In 5:11,15 we find a "prophecy" that there will be three eyewitnesses to the plates. There are many letters addressed by God or by Jesus giving specific instructions to people Joseph is having trouble with. For example, 5:23 is a command to Martin Harris (one of the three witnesses) to be more humble and repent. In Section 7 we learn that the apostle John was told by Jesus that he would in fact not die (which anticipates the Mormon teaching that he is still alive today).

In *D&C* 9, Oliver Cowdery is told to keep helping Joseph with the translation. He is told that there are "other records" besides the plates of Nephi which will be revealed (9:2), but from now on, he will write only for Joseph. He will not be allowed to translate or to have his own revelations. In *D&C* 10, Joseph is given a reason that the 116 manuscript pages of the Book of Mormon stolen by Martin Harris' wife will not be retranslated. We can assume that this "revelation" was given because, if he was to retranslate the pages and Mrs. Harris was to produce the earlier "translations," the fraud of the supposedly inspired translation would be uncovered. Instead, in *D&C* 10, Joseph is told that he should not retranslate because Satan will inspire the person holding the 116 pages to alter them. In 10:59-60 is an interesting interpretation of a New Testament passage. We learn that the "other sheep I have, but not of this sheep pen" in John 10:16 are Mormons! If we read John 10:16, Jesus is referring to future disciples who are Gentiles, certainly not to Mormons.

*D&C* 13 is an important one. It is here the revelation is given that Joseph Smith will restore the "Aaronic Priesthood." This command comes from John the Baptist. "I confer the priesthood of Aaron on you, which holds the keys of the ministering of angels and of the gospel of repentance and baptism by immersion for the remission of sins" (13:1). In 17:1 we learn that the three witnesses to the golden plates are Oliver Cowdery, Martin Harris and David Whitmer (all of whom later left the movement). They are told that they will see the plates, as well as the sword of Laban and the Urim and Thummim "by faith." In 19:22 Mormons are told to deliver "milk not meat" to the people. In other words, for those they evangelize, they are not to tell all the Mormon teachings, but only the command to repent and be baptized. This advice is now a standard part of Mormon practice. Members are told to only reveal the simplest and least controversial teachings to those they are recruiting. If asked about more controversial topics, they are trained to change the subject. In 19:26 we find the first of many revelations that converts should not "covet" their own property (an interesting interpretation of the word covet), but should impart it freely to the church. In this case, Martin Harris is commanded to sell his property and to use the money to print the Book of Mormon. *D&C* 20 is another important section. Here are laid out the principal organization of church hierarchical offices. We are informed that those who do not accept the Book of Mormon will be condemned (20:15). The Lord's Supper includes bread and wine (20:40) (the LDS church uses bread and water today). We learn that the Holy Ghost is imparted, not when one is baptized (Acts 2:38, 5:32), but by the laying on of hands (20:43). Offices in the Mormon Church will be apostle, elder and priest (who can baptize), as well as teacher and deacon (who cannot baptize). *D&C* 21 is considered the point at which the Latter-day Saint Church was actually begun and salvation was granted to mankind for the first time in more than 1300 years. According to the Mormons, Joseph officially revived the Christian church on April 6, 1830.

In *D&C* 25:4, Emma Smith is commanded not to complain that she cannot be shown the golden plates, and that she is to be a scribe when Oliver Cowdery is not available. We learn that the biblical Adam is the Archangel Michael (27:14). In Section 28 is the command that only Joseph Smith (not Hiram Page) can receive visions using stones, and Hiram is commanded to go to Ohio to preach to the Lamanites. This example is one of many in *D&C* where those exhibiting insubordination to Smith are commanded by God to go on long missionary trips. We learn that the New Jerusalem, Zion is "on the border of the Lamanites" (*D&C* 32). Sidney Rigdon is commissioned to work miracles in 35:20. The doctrine of the reestablished Zion/city of Enoch is revealed in 38:4 and 45:11. Section 44 is one of many commanding that the poor and needy should be taken care of. To be fair to Mormons and to their religion, this is an admirable part of their teaching, and one that they have often practiced more extensively than their more orthodox Christian neighbors. In 45:60 Joseph Smith is commanded to translate the New Testament, despite the fact that he had no knowledge of Greek. In 49:16 the revelation is given that a man can have only one wife. This commandment was supposedly given to Joseph in 1831, yet it contradicts Section 132, where we are told that Joseph had been given knowledge of the plural marriage doctrine in 1831.

Joseph is told that the property of anyone who leaves the church cannot be received back by the person who leaves (51:5). This provided strong motivation for people not to apostatize. In Section 57 we learn that the New Jerusalem is to be established in Independence, Missouri. "The place which is now called Independence is the center place; and a spot for the temple is lying westward on a lot which is not far from the courthouse" (57:3). It is an "everlasting inheritance" (57:5). We know from other sources that Joseph designated the exact spot where the temple would be built. This prophecy has still not been fulfilled, although the Reformed Latter-day Saints did repurchase the property. For the first generation or so of those in Salt Lake City, it was assumed that the church would eventually return in triumph to occupy Independence, Missouri. Eventually, this claim stopped being voiced by the Utah Mormons. Section

68 is also noteworthy. Here Joseph claims to have been told to reestablish the Priesthood of Melchizedek (68:15). "Literal direct descendants of Aaron" are priests of this order automatically (68:19). We are told later that only members of the Melchizedek priesthood have a secure place in the highest level of heaven. In 72:13 is the first use of the significant Mormon expression, "in time and eternity." Also in this section the Latter-day Saints in Missouri are told that Mormons must give up all their money and possessions to the church (72:15). This was later rescinded.

At this point (February 1832), Joseph became bolder. He began to introduce radical new teachings, many of which could be considered sub-Christian or heretical. Section 76 is one of the most important in D&C in this regard. It is here that we first learn of the three levels of heaven and the three kingdoms of God: celestial, terrestrial, and telestial. We learn that while "translating" the New Testament, Smith and Sidney Rigdon came to understand that part of the gospel of John (at John 5:29) has been removed. Apparently, this is where Jesus spoke of the three kingdoms of God. There is no manuscript evidence to support this claim. Smith learns that there are many inhabited worlds with sons and daughters of God (76:24). He is told that those who leave Mormonism will go to hell. Those who never became Mormons do not go to hell, but to the telestial kingdom. In other words, those who convert to Mormonism but leave are far worse off than those who never were converted (76:31–38). This teaching is one of the reasons it is so hard to "convert" people away from Mormonism. Virtual universalism (salvation of all souls) is taught, as only those who leave the church will go to hell (76:39–48). The members of the Melchizedek priesthood and the Order of Enoch will be in the celestial kingdom (7:50). Those in the highest, celestial kingdom "are gods, even the sons of God" (76:58). Here we find for the first time what may be the most controversial theological claim of Mormonism. Those in the celestial kingdom have "celestial bodies" (76:70). The terrestrial kingdom is described (76:71–79). Its occupants are those "whose glory differs from that of the church of the Firstborn who have received the fullness of the Father, even as that of the moon differs from the sun in the firmament." These "died without law," and are saved by repenting and receiving Jesus in Hades, but not in this life. They are "honorable men of the earth who were blinded by the craftiness of men" (76:75). They occupy terrestrial bodies and see the Son but not the Father (7:78). Next, the telestial kingdom is described (76:81–101). The glory of those in the telestial kingdom is to those in the terrestrial as the glory of the stars is to that of the moon. Its subjects did not receive the gospel of Christ or the testimony of Jesus. "These are they who are of Paul, and of Apollos and of Cephas"—a reference to 1 Corinthians 1:12, in which Paul teaches against divisiveness in the church (76:99). The implication is that those in denominational churches will be in the telestial kingdom. Those is the third kingdom will serve God, "but not where God and Christ dwell" (76:112).

In *D&C* 77:7 we learn that there will be a 7000-year reign of Christ. Returning to revelations about the three kingdoms of God, Joseph reveals that those in the celestial kingdom will be rulers over many in the city of Adam-ondi-Ahman (78:15). Later, Orson Pratt explained that this term is part of the Adamic language.[93] After much expectation on the part of his followers, Joseph revealed that "Zion"—the New Jerusalem—will be established in Independence, Missouri (84:4). The temple will be built there within a generation (a prophecy which was not fulfilled). In this section we find a number of examples of poor spelling and grammar, such as the word "athirst," and the expressions "for thus it seemeth me good," and "clearly and understandingly." In *D&C* 87 we find a prophecy of a great war over slavery "that will shortly come to pass" between "all nations" (87:2). The war will begin in South Carolina (87:1). This is the most famous of Smith's prophecies, and is used by his followers as evidence he is an inspired teacher.

Section 88 contains more discussion of the three kingdoms. The celestial body is a natural, physical body with flesh and bones (7:28). There are many kingdoms and many planets, each with a kingdom of its own (7:37). This suggests the Mormon doctrine that those in the celestial kingdom can progress to being a god of a planet of their own.

Section 89 is the famous "Word of Wisdom." This is the advice on healthy living for which the LDS are well known. It is given as a strong advice—a "word of wisdom"—but not a commandment. Saints are advised to abstain from alcohol, tobacco, and hot drinks (later interpreted to imply caffeine-containing drinks), and to avoid eating too much meat.

Section 93 of *D&C* is important. Here we learn of what is known as the doctrine of "eternal progression." In this case, Joseph Smith is supposedly channeling the words of the apostle John. We are told that, like us, Jesus was not "full" at first (93:14), but that he became full and received the fullness of glory at his baptism (93:15–16). If a member of the Melchizedek priesthood is sufficiently faithful, he too will receive the same glory as Jesus (93:18). We will be glorified in Jesus as Jesus is glorified in the Father (93:20).

In Section 97, as elsewhere, the Saints are advised not to retaliate against their persecutors. In Section 101 they are told that they are being forced out of Independence, Missouri because of their sins, but that they will return to Zion. God will not choose another place (101:18–20). This prophecy is yet to be fulfilled. In Section 103 the Mormons in Kirtland are ordered to form "Zion's Camp," which is the band of Mormon soldiers who went to Missouri to fight for those persecuted there. They are told that the Saints will win the battle (103:6), which did not come to pass. Later, in Section 104, Joseph admits that Zion's Camp was defeated, telling the discouraged that "I am trying to test your faith" (104:19). In 107:19 we learn that those in the Melchizedek priesthood will be in the celestial kingdom, and that the priesthood is inherited from father to son (107:40–41). This revelation is significant to the dispute over who would succeed Joseph Smith with possession of the "keys to the kingdom." If this command was strictly observed, then Brigham Young would not have succeeded to the Mormon presidency. Section 111 is an embarrassing one, as it relates to Joseph Smith's treasure hunt trip to Salem, Massachusetts. "I have much treasure in this city [Salem]" (111:2). The treasure Joseph will discover there will take care of the debt problem raised by the banking scandal in Kirtland. Joseph is told that he will find gold there left behind by more ancient inhabitants (111:9). Given how the expedition turned out, it is a bit surprising that this revelation has not been expunged from *D&C*.

In Section 115, Joseph is told that from now on the church he is reestablishing will be the Church of Jesus Christ of Latter-day Saints. Then in Section 116 Joseph reveals that a location near Far West, Missouri is Adam-ondi-Ahman—the location of the place where Adam will come to visit his people. Adam is the "Ancient of Days." In other words, Adam is God. In 124:29 the doctrine of baptism of living Saints for the dead is revealed. Such "sealings" can only be performed in a temple, under the authority of the President and Prophet of the church. In this section, the Mormons are instructed to build the Nauvoo House, where Joseph and his family can live from generation to generation (124:56). Also, Brigham Young is named the head of the twelve apostles (124:127).

At this point (1842), Smith's oracles change from the third person to the first person. Smith proclaims to his followers directly. The novel doctrines proposed by Smith also become bolder. As already stated, Smith has now become sufficiently confident of his followers' faith in his authority that he feels he can speak directly for God, rather than being the channel through which God or another exalted person speaks. We find the famous statement of Joseph about himself, "Deep water is what I am wont to swim in. It has all become second nature to me; and I feel like Paul, to glory in tribulation" (127:2). In 128 he gives more instruction on baptism for the dead. This ceremony is "for the salvation of the dead who should die without knowledge of the gospel" (128:5). We are told by Smith that in Revelation 20:12, John was anticipating the teaching of baptism for the dead (128:6). Further, Malachi 4:5–6, where the Lord tells us that Elijah "will turn the hearts of the fathers to their children, and the hearts of the children to their fathers" is a reference to baptism for the dead (128:17). Here is intimated the doctrine of spiritual families in heaven—that having celestial wives, parents and children is key to our glorification. "We without them cannot be made perfect; neither can they without us be made perfect" (128:18).

Next, we learn that there are two different final states for people in heaven, and that not all souls will be resurrected. (Mormons teach that our physical body is part of our soul). Some will exist as spirits, while others will have physical, flesh-and-blood bodies. The spirits in heaven are "just men made perfect," but who were not resurrected (129:3). Angels are resurrected people and therefore have flesh-and-blood bodies (129:5). Then Smith offers a shocking teaching: Jesus has a flesh-and-blood body in heaven (130:1), and God the Father also has a flesh-and-blood body (130:3). God's reckoning of time, as well as that of angels and prophets, depends on the planet on which they live (130:4). The planet where God the Father resides is a massive Urim and Thummim (130:8)! Eventually, Christ will rule over the earth (130:9). Smith informs us, using Revelation 2:17 as evidence, that each of us (assuming that we are part of the Melchizedek priesthood) can have our own Urim and Thummim (139:10). The implication is that we, as gods, can rule over our own planet as we progress in our godhood. Reiterating what he has already said, Joseph ends this section emphatically by telling us that the Father has a body of flesh and bones as tangible as that of man's (130:32).

As shocking as this revelation is, the next two sections of the *Doctrine and Covenants* are the most notorious of all. This is where Joseph finally publicly revealed what he had taught and practiced since 1831—plural marriage. In the section notes to *D&C* 132 the church acknowledges that, "it is evident from the historical records that the doctrines and principles involved in this revelation had been known by the Prophet since 1831." There are three degrees of glory in the celestial kingdom (131:1). The highest level is only attainable to those who are sealed in marriage in a Mormon temple (131:2–5, 132:18–19), and only those on this level can progress to become gods. We are also informed here that "All spirit is matter" (131:7). Abraham, Isaac, David and others were justified by having multiple wives (132:1). Polygamous, plural, "celestial" marriages are a new and everlasting covenant (132:4). These celestial marriages are sealed "for time and eternity" in a temple ceremony (132:7). Marriage which is not "sealed" in a temple is only "for time," and is invalid in heaven (132:15). Those without a sealed celestial marriage can be saved, but they cannot progress to godhood. Joseph reveals about those with a celestial marriage "they shall pass by the angels and the gods, which are set there, to their exaltation and glory in all things as hath been sealed upon their heads" (132:19). "Then shall they be gods... then shall they be above all" (132:20). Mormons are commanded, "go ye and do the works of Abraham" (take plural wives) (132:32). Moses is exalted because he had multiple wives (132:38). (There is no biblical evidence that Moses had more than one wife). Anticipating the shock that Emma Smith would feel at this revelation, the prophet has her commanded to "receive all those that have been given unto my servant Joseph (132:52). If not, she will be destroyed" (132:54).

Joseph is justified even if he has ten wives (132:62).

In Section 135 is an account by John Taylor of the death of Joseph and Hyrum Smith. The account fails to mention that Joseph died with a gun in his hand, which he unloaded at the mob which came to kill him. Brigham Young inserts a single section (136) with instructions for the pioneers on the way to Salt Lake. Section 138 is a revelation from Joseph F. Smith, nephew of Joseph Smith, Jr., revealed in 1918, which explains the Manifesto concerning polygamy of 1890 and confirms the already-accepted Mormon doctrine of the pre-existence of souls (138:56). This is followed by the Official Declaration, also known as the Manifesto of October 11, 1890 in which Mormon president Wilford Woodruff announces that plural marriages will no longer be performed in Mormon temples. Lastly, a second Official Declaration of 1978 is appended. This is the one in which the church announced that it will begin to accept blacks into the Aaronic and Melchizedek priesthoods.

## The Pearl of Great Price

The final addition to the official Latter-day-Saint scriptural canon was first published in 1851. It was accepted as a standard work of the church under the title *The Pearl of Great Price* (Pearl) in 1880. The text consists of a number of relatively short works. The first is *Selections from the Book of Moses*. This is an extract of the "translation" of the Old Testament made by Joseph Smith in 1830–31. The second is the *Book of Abraham*. This is the material that Joseph claimed to be an inspired translation of the Egyptian papyri that came into his possession while in Kirtland in 1835. The third section is a small piece of Smith's "translation" of the New Testament. It is his version of Matthew 23:39–24:51. Next comes a piece titled *Joseph Smith—History*, which is a section of the *History of the Church*, written by Joseph Smith. The account is intended to explain his call by God, his acquisition of the golden plates and the process of translation. Last comes a brief document titled *The Articles of Faith*. This could be described as a Mormon creed. We will proceed to a brief analysis of the various parts of *The Pearl of Great Price*.

## Moses

*Selections from the Book of Moses* is more commonly known simply as *Moses*. It was first produced by Joseph Smith in June 1830. It was originally part of his "translation" of the Old Testament. The Utah Mormon Church has never published this translation and has discouraged its being published by others. When Smith died, the Quorum of the Twelve asked Emma for the manuscript, but she refused. Later, in 1867, the Reformed Church of Jesus Christ of Latter-day Saints (RLDS) published Joseph's entire translation of the King James Bible. The word translation is used loosely here because there is no evidence that Joseph had any knowledge of Hebrew, the primary original language of the Old Testament. When one reads the text of Moses, it is apparent that it is both a revision and an interpolation of the King James Version from the first several chapters of Genesis. Therefore it is best called a revision rather than a translation.

*Moses* begins with a long interpolation (addition) to Genesis that purports to be the story of how God spoke to Moses. Apparently, Smith believed that Moses actually wrote the book of Genesis, although some would consider the evidence for Mosaic authorship slim. When one reads *Moses*, it is not hard to guess the identity of its real author. The phrase "and it came to pass" is used dozens of times in a fairly short document. It would be quite a coincidence if the only two authors of scripture to use the phrase "and it came to pass" were Nephi and Moses, but that Moses stopped using this phrase in the parts of Genesis that were left unchanged by Smith. A more reasonable conclusion is that Joseph Smith is the original author of the Book of Mormon and of the interpolations to Genesis found in the *Pearl*.

In *Moses* chapter one Moses sees God on a great mountain. He is told that he is a prefigure (similitude) of "mine only Begotten" (1:6,13). Like Jesus, Moses is tempted by Satan in the desert, on a mountain (1:12–21). We are told that the material we are reading was removed from the original book we now know as Genesis "because of wickedness" (1:23). Moses learns that there are many earths, each inhabited: "And worlds without number have I created" (1:29,33). We find a prophecy that God will raise up Joseph Smith after men who do not esteem God will have taken many of the words out of the book of Genesis. The implication is that Joseph is the one to restore the parts of the scripture that were removed. There is no textual evidence to support the claim that "wicked people" removed parts of Genesis. Moses is told, "Behold, I will raise up another like unto thee" (1:41). In Moses this is a reference to Joseph Smith, whereas in Deuteronomy 18 God says something similar to Moses which we know is a prophecy of the Messiah, not Smith (see Acts 3:22–26).[94]

Material with parallels to Genesis begins in *Moses* chapter two. An interpolation describing Satan's fall is given (4:1–4). Adam receives the "Holy Ghost" in *Moses* 5:9. It is a good thing that Adam sinned: "Because of my transgression my eyes are opened and in this life I shall have joy and again in the flesh I shall see God" (5:10). If it were not for their transgression, Adam and Eve would not have had seed and therefore the eternal life that God offers (5:11). Cain gives orders to Satan and is called Master Mahan (5:31). Humans were created in the image of God's own body. In other words, our being created in the image of God includes having a physical body like his (6:9).

At this point, *Moses* takes a bizarre turn. Adam preaches belief, repentance and baptism "in the name of the Only Begotten Son who is full of grace and truth which is Jesus Christ" (6:52). Those who accepted his message became part of the children of men and received the gift of the Holy Ghost. This takes the anachronistic teaching about Jesus found in the Book of Mormon to new levels. The doctrine of original sin is refuted (6:54). We must be "born again... of water and of the Spirit" (6:59). Adam is baptized (6:64).

Next, we have a speech by Enoch. He tells us that the children of Canaan are cursed with blackness and despised among all people (7:8). Once again Smith's racist ideas surface. Enoch commanded people to be baptized in the name of the Father, the Son and the Holy Ghost (but he did not preach to black people) (7:11). Enoch builds a city called Zion. The city is taken up into heaven and a remnant are saved (7:18). Enoch's Zion will be a future gathering place for God's people (7:62). We can see Joseph placing his doctrine of the New Jerusalem into the book of Genesis. Like Adam and Enoch, Noah preaches belief, repentance and baptism in the name of Jesus Christ, and people receive the Holy Ghost (8:24). This, despite the fact that Jesus said he must die and go away before the Holy Ghost can be given (John 14:15–26).

## The Book of Abraham

As mentioned previously, Joseph Smith produced *The Book of Abraham* by a claimed inspired interpretation of a set of Egyptian papyri that came into his possession in Kirtland, Ohio. He told his followers that some of the writing on one of the documents was written by Abraham himself. Another of the papyri was written by Joseph (the biblical patriarch, not Smith). Three facsimiles of these papyri are included in modern editions of *Pearl* (see facsimile above). The actual papyrus Joseph claimed to contain the writing of *Abraham* was rediscovered in a museum in 1967. When it was translated by scholars, they discovered that part of the text came from the *Egyptian Book of the Dead*. Another section comes from the *Book of Breathings*. It is public knowledge that Smith's translation is a hoax.

The *Book of Abraham* begins with a claim that Abraham was a high priest (Abraham 1:2). Demonstrating his geographical confusion, Smith has Egyptian priests making sacrifices on an altar built in Chaldea (Mesopotamia) (1:8). Priests of Elkanah try to offer Abraham as a sacrifice to their god (1:12, see facsimile above). Smith shows further confusion between things Egyptian and Babylonian (Chaldean); he has Potiphar's Hill in the land of Ur of Chaldea (1:20). The biblical Potiphar is an Egyptian who lived more than five hundred years after Abraham. Abraham tells us the Egyptians are descended from Ham and Egyptus, which means that which is forbidden. The implication is that they are black and therefore not eligible for the priesthood (1:22).

Abraham (Smith?) now turns to cosmological speculation. Abraham is given the Urim and Thummim (3:1). He has a vision of Kolob which is the greatest of all stars. It is near the throne of God (see facsimile 2, Abraham 3:3). Kolob rotates once every 1000 years. This is why for God, a day is like 1000 years. On each of the worlds governed by Kolob, time is reckoned by the period of its rotation. Kolob is inhabited by eternal gods, with lesser stars ruled by lesser beings (3:21–23). One of the gods says to the others that he will go down and create the earth from pre-existing material (3:24). Those who obey this particular God will have glory (will become gods) and those who do not will not keep their glory (3:25–26). The God of the earth asks whom he should send to this planet. One, "like unto the Son of Man" offers and is accepted. Another, presumably Satan, offers and is refused. He loses his "first estate" (3:27–28). This is the source of the Mormon teaching that Jesus and Satan are brothers. After this important decision, the gods proceed to organize and form the heavens and the earth (4:1f).

What are we to think of this cosmological and theological speculation? From a Christian perspective, this is serious error. If Mormons accept this teaching, then we have a right to say that they are not Christian. They are polytheists. In the *Book of Abraham* and *Doctrine and Covenants*, Smith taught that humans have the potential to be gods themselves through a process of eternal progression. This may resonate with New Age concepts, but it is not biblical Christianity.

## Joseph Smith—Matthew

The next little section in *The Pearl* is a revision by Joseph Smith of Matthew 23:39–24:51. It is a small part of Smith's revision of the King James New Testament. It ends with the statement, "And thus cometh the end of the wicked, according to the prophecy of Moses, saying: They shall be cut off from among the people; but the end of the earth is not yet, but by and by."

## Joseph Smith—History

Those who compiled *The Pearl of Great Price* chose to insert part of Joseph Smith's *History of the Church* into their officially accepted scripture. This is a semi-autobiographical sketch penned by Joseph. He produced his history as an apologetic to explain and defend his version of the events surrounding the formation of Mormonism. The most important content in this book has already been discussed in our sketch of the life of Joseph Smith. It includes one of the versions from Smith of his vision of the Father and the Son at the age of fourteen (1:17–20), including the command to not join any of the Christian denominations. Joseph confesses to sins in his youth, calling them "foibles of human nature" and declares himself not guilty of any great or malignant sins (1:28). He makes no mention of his treasure hunting or his arrest and conviction for "being a disorderly person and an imposter." *History* includes Smith's account of his second vision in 1823 in which Moroni supposedly told him in a triple vision about the golden plates, the Urim and Thummim and the sword of Laban which he had placed on the Hill Cumorah (1:30–47). Smith goes to see the plates but is forbidden to remove them. He returns every year on the same day until, four years later, in 1827, he is allowed to obtain the plates (1:59). Smith tells us that Emma's father opposed his marriage because of the vision he had received (1:58). We know from Isaac Hale that he opposed the marriage because Joseph was a shameless money-digger. We have already seen Eber D. Howe's version of Isaac's opinion of Joseph: "You spend your time in digging for money—pretending to see in a stone, and thus try to deceive people." Smith describes his translation of the golden plates. He tells us about Martin Harris' trip to New York with a facsimile of one of the plates, in an attempt to confirm their authenticity. Harris claims (1:64–65) that "Professor Anthon stated that the translation was correct, more so than any he had before seen translated from the Egyptian" (1:64). This is clearly not true, according to statements we have from Anthon himself. Smith also describes a vision in May 1829 in which John the Baptist restored the priesthood of Aaron and commanded that Smith and Oliver Cowdery be baptized (1:68–72).

## The Articles of Faith

*The Articles of Faith* can be described as a creed of Mormonism. There is relatively little controversial here. It includes a plan of salvation familiar from the other Mormon scriptures. Latter-day Saints are told that faith, repentance and baptism by immersion will lead to the forgiveness of sins, and that the laying on of hands will impart the gift of the Holy Ghost. The reality of modern-day miraculous gifts such as prophecy, revelation, visions, healings and the interpretation of tongues are affirmed. Mormons are told to anticipate more truths concerning the Kingdom of God. The future gathering of the Saints in a literal Zion (the New Jerusalem) on the American continent is affirmed.

## A Summary of Mormon Teachings

We want to summarize this chapter by highlighting the ideas and teachings unique to Mormonism which are not biblically supported. Compiling a list which is useful for Christians today requires a nuanced approach because different teachings of Smith and other Prophets of the LDS Church have a widely ranging level of authority to the Mormon believer.

First of all, some of the more radical teachings of Joseph Smith and his close associates are no longer supported by the Utah Mormons. (On the other hand, we will see in the next chapter that the Fundamentalist Latter-day Saints (FLDS) still hold to many of these teachings which the Utah Mormons have abandoned). There is another set of Mormon beliefs which have not been officially repudiated by the Latter-day Saints, but which most Mormons are either unaware or only vaguely aware of. We might want to be cautious about accusing people of holding to a teaching that they never even heard of. Another category of Mormon beliefs is those which were taught by Joseph Smith or his associates and generally accepted by the church, but which are not found in any of the officially accepted Mormon scriptures. In the list below we will quote some of these other sources.

Another distinction we want to make in the list below is between teachings that seem most basic to Christianity and those that are less essential to the faith. In the list below, some effort has been made to proceed from those Mormon teachings which seem to strike at the heart of Orthodox Christianity to those which are not relevant to the fundamental beliefs of the Christian Church. Some of the Mormon teachings listed below have been discussed sufficiently in the previous chapters that we will only list them and provide at least one reference. Others require discussion, especially if they are not found in the Book of Mormon, *D&C* or *Pearl*. All of these teachings and doctrines can be found throughout Mormon literature, but, when possible, we have chosen reference verses from within the accepted Mormon scriptures.

## Mormon Teachings

1. The Father, the Son and the Holy Ghost (using the term preferred by the Mormons) are three separate gods.

   Joseph Smith gave what is his most famous speech, known as the King Follett discourse, on April 7, 1844. In the speech he declared, "I will preach on the plurality of Gods. I have always declared God to be a distinct personage, Jesus Christ a separate and distinct personage from God the Father, and the Holy Ghost was a distinct personage and a Spirit: and these three constitute three distinct personages and three Gods."[95]

2. There are many gods. *D&C* 76:58, *Abraham* 3.

3. The Father and the Son, in heaven, have physical flesh-and-blood bodies. *D&C* 130:1–3, 32.

4. Eternal progression. Humans in the highest level of the celestial kingdom can be glorified and become gods, eventually even being over a planet of their own. *D&C* 93, 139:10, *Abraham* 3.

   In April 1844, Joseph Smith preached his most famous sermon in front of an estimated crowd of 20,000. "God himself was once as we are now, and is an exalted man, and sits enthroned in yonder heavens!... I am going to tell you how God came to be God. We have imagined and supposed that God was God from all eternity. I will refute that idea, and take away the veil so that you may see... He was once a man like us; yea that God himself, the Father of us all, dwelt on an earth, the same as Jesus Christ himself did...Here, then is eternal life... you have got to learn how to be Gods yourselves,...the same as all Gods have done before you."[96]

5. Adam is the Archangel Michael and he is God the Father. *D&C* 116.

   When our father Adam came into the garden of Eden, he came into it with a celestial body, and brought Eve, one of his wives, with him. He helped to make and organize this world. He is Michael, the Archangel, the Ancient of Days! About whom holy men have written and spoken. He is our Father and our God, and the only God with whom we have to do."[97]

6. Jesus and Satan were spiritual brothers. *Abraham* 3:25–28.

   Milton Hunter of the Council of the Seventy said, "The appointment of Jesus to be the Savior of the world was contested by one of the other sons of God. He was called Lucifer, son of the morning. Haughty, ambitious, and covetous of power and glory, this spirit-brother of Jesus desperately tried to become the Savior of mankind."[98]

7. God has a mother—our Mother in Heaven.

   The doctrine of a Heavenly Mother is still found in Mormonism today. Early Mormon teachers traced the teaching back to Joseph Smith, although we do not find it stated directly in his writings. That Smith originated this teaching is implied in the official Latter-day Saint church history which quotes Smith as saying, "Come to me; here's the mysteries man hath not seen, Here's our Father in heaven, and Mother, the Queen."[99] Brigham Young said that he "would not worship a God who had not a father; and I do not know that he would if he had not a mother; the one would be as absurd as the other."[100]

8. There was a complete falling away of the Church soon after apostolic times. Joseph Smith reestablished the Kingdom of God on earth in 1830. *D&C* 21.

9. Revived Levitical Priesthood. *D&C* 13:1f.

10. Revived Melchizedek Priesthood. *D&C* 68:15f.

11. Three Kingdoms of God: the celestial, terrestrial and telestial. *D&C* 76.

12. Baptism for the dead. *D&C* 124:29, 128.

13. Pre-existence of human souls that determines their station in life. *D&C* 138:56.

    In April, 1844, Smith taught:

    "[T]he soul—the mind of man—the immortal spirit. Where did it come from? All learned men and doctors of divinity say that God created it in the beginning; but it is not so: the very idea lessens man in my estimation.... We say that God himself is a self-existent being.... Man does exist upon the same principles.... [The Bible] does not say in the Hebrew that God created the spirit of man. It says 'God made man out of the earth and put into him Adam's spirit, and so became a living body.' The mind or the intelligence which man possesses is co-equal with God himself.... Is it logical to say that the intelligence of spirits is immortal, and yet that it had a beginning? The intelligence of spirits had not beginning, neither will it have an end. That is good logic. That which has a beginning may have an end. There never was a time when there were not spirits; for they are co-equal [co-eternal] with our Father in heaven."[101]

14. Celestial (eternal) marriage, celestial families. Still believed by Mormons, although its sister doctrine polygamy has been abandoned. *D&C* 131, 132

15. Plural marriage (polygamy). Not officially practiced by the Utah church since 1890. *D&C* 131, 132.

    Mormon apostle and later counselor to Brigham Young in the church's First Presidency Jedediah M. Grant said, "The grand reason why the gentiles and philosophers of his school persecuted Jesus Christ, was because he had so many wives; there were Elizabeth, and Mary, and a host of others that followed him." He goes on to say, "The grand reason of the burst of public sentiment in anathemas upon Christ and his disciples, causing crucifixion, was evidently based upon polygamy, according to the testimony of the philosophers who rose in that age. A belief in the plurality of wives caused the persecution of Jesus and his followers. We might almost think they were 'Mormons'"[102]

16. Nearly everyone goes to one of three levels of heaven: the celestial, terrestrial or telestial (this was described as virtual Universalism above). *D&C* 76.

17. Miracles such as modern day revelation, prophecies, tongues, etc. are still in effect. *Articles of the Faith* 7.

18. Blood atonement. As mentioned above, this was taught openly by Brigham Young and Orson and Parley Pratt.[103] It is not clear that Joseph Smith taught this. This doctrine is no longer held to by the Mormon Church.

19. Jesus was conceived through God having sexual relations with Mary. This makes God the Father a polygamist. Most modern Mormons do not accept this belief.

    Brigham Young said, "That very babe that was cradled in the manger was begotten, not by Joseph, the husband of Mary, but by another Being. Do you inquire by whom? He was begotten by God our heavenly Father, by the process known to nature—just as men now create children.[104]

    He also said, "When our father Adam came into the Garden of Eden he came into it with a celestial body, and brought Eve, one of his wives, with him. He helped to make and organize this world. He is Michael, the Archangel, the Ancient of Days! About whom holy men have written and spoken—He is our Father and our God, and the only God with whom we have to do."[105]

20. People with darker skins are cursed—especially blacks. *Moses* 7:8–11, *Abraham* 1:22. Blacks and especially Indians are degenerate humans. Mormon 5:15. "Indians are dark filthy and loathsome" (1 Neph 11:13). "Dark people are sinful" (2 Nephi 5:21). Dark skin is loathsome. Those who marry the dark skinned are cursed. Blacks were only admitted to the Levitical and Melchizedek priesthoods upon a later revelation in 1979. *D&C* 139.

21. The Book of Mormon, *Doctrines and Covenants* and *The Pearl of Great Price* are inspired by God. *Articles of Faith* 8.

22. Joseph Smith is a prophet, seer and revelator.

23. There are many planets, with advanced spiritual beings—gods—over them. *D&C* 93, *Moses* 1:23, 29, 33.

24. Physical bodies are soul. *D&C* 131:7

25. God's throne is near the great star Kolob which rotates every 1000 years. *Abraham* 3:1f.

26. The universe is formed of pre-existing material. The physical universe is eternal. *Abraham* 3:24.

27. Zion—the New Jerusalem—will be reestablished in Independence, Missouri. *D&C* 38:4, 45:11, 57:3–5, *Moses* 7:62.

28. "Great and precious promises" have been removed by wicked men from the Bible, so that it is not complete, which is why the Book of Mormon is needed. 1 Nephi 13:26–27.

# Chapter 8

# Modern Mormonism

All of us have known Mormons personally. To some extent, they are a mystery to us. If this group has such strange teachings, how can we explain the fact that the Mormon Church is one of the fastest growing religious groups in the world? Why is it that Mormons, on the outside, appear more "Christian" than the typical Christian we meet? What goes on in those secret temple rites? What's up with the weird underwear? We have heard about some really strange beliefs of the Mormons. Does the average member actually believe these things? In this chapter we will attempt to address these and other questions about modern Mormonism as lived and practiced today.

We will start with some facts about the Church of Jesus Christ of Latter-day Saints. After their phenomenal rate of growth in the mid-1800s the Utah Mormons have grown more slowly, but their growth has been remarkably consistent. This makes the Mormon Church an anomaly. Most successful religious groups experience initial rapid growth, followed by a period of slower growth, then by a period of equilibrium, and later steady decline. After 180 years, the Mormons remain in the second phase, with no obvious signs of that ending. Growth at a steady rate by percentage-per-year is called exponential growth. To date, the LDS Church has experienced exponential growth. Since 1860, the yearly growth rate of the LDS church has held at a remarkably stable level of 3.5–4%. If we look at the history of Mormon membership we will see this clearly illustrated (see end note).[106]

Since 1995, the growth has decreased slightly, to less than 3%. However, if compared to any other major religious group, this is still impressive. Worldwide Mormon membership will surpass 15 million in 2012. Of those, just over six million are in the United States and just under nine million are outside the country. Membership in the United States has nearly plateaued—with most "growth" coming from the baptism of children of the members. The real growth of the church is occurring principally in foreign countries, where the Mormons have their missions. In 2009 there were 280,000 baptisms in the church, there were 51,736 full-time missionaries and there were 130 temples in operation.[107]

How do we explain the growth of the church? It seems that the main statistic shedding light on this question is the number of full-time missionaries. The Mormon Church has built up a missionary program that is the envy of many religious groups. There are other factors in the growth, but surely the laserlike focus of the entire worldwide Mormon network to train, support and send out missionaries is the primary factor ensuring steady growth of the movement. Any follower of Christ reading this book should take note of this fact.

How do they maintain such an effective missionary program? First, it is part of the Mormon culture. From their earliest years, Mormon children are saturated with the idea that a good Mormon will put in two years of missionary service. They are told at an impressionable age that their place in the celestial kingdom will be both secured and improved by going on a mission. They understand that afterwards they will settle down with a faithful Mormon wife to raise children and build a celestial family. When they come home from the mission trip, their work of evangelizing will be essentially done. They can settle down to life in a secure, accepting, supportive community. Because of the strong family and community support system, this expectation of a financially secure future is no pipe dream.

Another reason for the success of their missionary programs is that the LDS Church is willing to devote time, effort and, perhaps most significantly, *money* to build up a truly world-class missionary program. The families of the missionaries are asked to contribute to the cost, but still the missionaries are largely subsidized by the church. The prospective missionary is given up to a full year of training, including indoctrination in the teachings of Mormonism and study of a foreign language. Boys go on their two-year mission at about nineteen years of age. Girls, who comprise a much smaller part of the missionaries, go at about twenty to twenty-one years.

Sustaining a strong missionary program requires a lot of money. The LDS is a wealthy church. Its net worth has been estimated to be about 30 billion dollars, with the value of its businesses and corporations about 100 billion dollars.[108] It has money to spend on evangelization. Members are required to give a tithe (a true tithe, or 10%) of their gross income. Such giving is mandated through regular personal interviews. Furthermore, nearly all local ministry staff of the Latter-day Saints is unpaid. Local wards or branches are led by a "bishop," who is a member of the Melchizedek priesthood. He serves for four to seven years and is unpaid. Moreover, nearly all Mormon functions are supported fully by volunteers. Mormons are told that they gain higher ultimate standing in the celestial kingdom by such service. Levels of service are monitored by local bishops, and advancement in the priesthood is based on one's level of service.

Imagine a church in which the members faithfully gave 10% of their income *and* the money was not needed to pay church staff! This, among other factors, is why the LDS church is able to support both the construction of impressive temples and a highly effective missionary program. How and whether Christians ought to consider applying such a model to their mission of saving the lost is something that deserves thought and consideration.

The principal goal of this chapter is to understand how our Mormon friend "ticks." We will need to understand Mormon culture and the dynamics of power in the temples.

## Mormon Temple Ceremonies

We have purposefully delayed discussion of Mormon temple ceremonies for this chapter on modern Mormonism. One cannot understand the mindset of Mormons without considering their ceremonies and, most important, the effect those ceremonies have on the thinking and actions of a faithful believer. The "endowments" (see below) can only be performed at a Mormon gemple, of which there are over 130 now in operation. From earliest youth Mormons anticipate their initiation into the temple rites. Those who live at some distance from a temple participate in "temple excursions" in groups, like a class trip for endowments and baptisms for the dead.

There are several kinds of endowment ceremonies performed in Mormon temples. The most important are:

1. Washings and anointings
2. Endowment into the priesthood (symbolically "passing through the veil" to the highest level of heaven)
3. Eternal marriage (which can be performed, like proxy baptisms, for the dead)
4. Sealing ceremonies (children born to parents who were not LDS at the time of their birth can be "sealed" to them so that they are part of their celestial family)
5. Proxy baptisms for the dead

We will focus principally on the priesthood endowment ceremony and proxy baptisms, as these form such an essential part of how Mormons view themselves as different from all other people.

The endowment ceremony is generally performed on men just before they go on their mission, at nineteen years of age. For women, it is done before they go on a mission or, more commonly, immediately before their marriage. For converts to Mormonism, the endowment occurs at least six months after their baptism. For those raised in the church, their first ceremony is a kind of coming-of-age. They are now part of a secret world that even their own parents have never shared with them.

In the past few years, the endowment ceremony has become far less secret. Anyone who wants to is able to find YouTube videos of reenactments by former Mormons of all or part of the temple ceremonies.

Before any male or female Mormon can undergo a sealing, an endowment, a celestial marriage or a proxy baptism, he or she must undergo an interview at which the correct answers must be given to a number of questions. It is their anticipation of the answers they will give to these questions which governs to a great extent how the Mormons live their daily lives. A Mormon considering drinking coffee, whether or not to wear the special clothing, how much work to put into church service, or whether to have sex outside marriage knows that he or she will be answering questions about these things face-to-face before a bishop, and that their ability to progress toward godhood is determined by these interviews. Those who successfully complete this interview are given a recommendation from the local ward or branch that qualifies them to travel to a temple and go through a ceremony. It is difficult to overestimate the influence of the anticipation of these interviews on a practicing Mormon. As we look below at the list of questions in the interview and later at the detailed ceremony, we may conclude that the interview is even more crucial to maintaining control of Mormon believers than the endowment ceremonies themselves. Their effect is to reinforce Mormon morality, loyalty to Mormon leadership and, most especially, the role of testimony in maintaining commitment to the Mormon religion. For this reason, we include the questions in full:

1. Do you have faith in and a testimony of God, the Eternal Father, his Son Jesus Christ, and the Holy Ghost?
2. Do you have a testimony of the Atonement of Christ and of his role as Savior and Redeemer?
3. Do you have a testimony of the restoration of the gospel in these latter days?
4. Do you sustain the President of the Church of Jesus Christ of Latter-day Saints as the Prophet, Seer and Revelator and as the only person on the earth who possesses and is authorized to exercise all the priesthood keys?

   Do you sustain members of the First Presidency and the Quorum of the Twelve Apostles as prophets, seers and revelators? Do you sustain the other General

Authorities and local authorities of the Church?

5. Do you live by the law of chastity?
6. Is there anything in your conduct relating to the members of your family that is not in harmony with the teachings of the Church?
7. Do you support, affiliate with, or agree with any group or individual whose teachings or practices are contrary to or oppose those accepted by the Church of Jesus Christ of Latter-day Saints?
8. Do you strive to keep the covenants you have made, to attend your sacrament and other meetings, and to keep your life in harmony with the laws and commandments of the gospel?
9. Are you honest in your dealings with your fellowmen?
10. Are you a full-tithe payer?
11. Do you keep the Word of Wisdom?
12. Do you have financial or other obligations to a former spouse or children? If yes, are you current in meeting those obligations?
13. [Assuming a previous endowment] Do you keep the covenants that you made in the temple? Do you wear the garment both night and day as instructed in the endowment and in accordance with the covenant you made in the temple?
14. Have there been any sins or misdeeds in your life that should have been resolved with priesthood authorities but have not been?
15. Do you consider yourself worthy to enter the Lord's house and participate in temple ordinances?

It is chilling to think of the intellectual mind control behind question 7. Bear in mind that the person performing this interview is the bishop of the local ward and will have some firsthand knowledge of how truthful the one making this pledge is being.

## The Endowment Ceremony

Upon arriving at the temple for a secret ceremony the participant submits his or her recommendation from a local ward bishop, as well as his or her four-generation pedigree (or the pedigree of those for whom they are undergoing vicarious baptism). The ceremony which they then embark on takes about five hours. Below is a description of the endowment ceremony adapted from one published by former Mormon Latayne Scott.[109]

The endowees first dress in the one-piece undergarment they will wear for the rest of their life (except for sporting events). The garment goes to just below the knee and well above the waist. It includes a picture of a compass, a square, as well as a mark in the navel area and on the knees (virtually identical to those used in Masonic ceremonies). Songs are sung, passages are read, and symbolic washings are performed. A line is drawn by a worker (a member of the Melchizedek priesthood serving in the temple) across the candidate's forehead with a wet finger. The worker reads a list of the parts of the body purified by this washing: the head, nose, lips, neck, shoulders, back, breast, "vitals," "bowels," arms, hands, "loins," legs and feet. In the past, all these parts were touched by the one performing the ceremony (no longer the custom). A rote "sealing" formula is read by another worker. Both lay their hands on the head of the participant. The endowee is next moved to another area. The sealing worker puts a drop of oil on the head, and recites a list of the same body parts as before. Another sealing formula is read and hands are laid on again. The candidate then moves to a third area. A statement is read "authorizing" the undergarment. The participants are told that this garment represents that given to Adam in the Garden of Eden and is a "garment of the holy priesthood," which will be a "shield of protection" to the wearer until death.

At this point the endowee is given a secret "new name"—usually a biblical or Book of Mormon name—by the temple worker. He is told not to reveal this name to anyone except in later temple ceremonies. The man knows his new name and that of his wife, but the wife does not know the secret name of her husband because women cannot be members of the priesthood.

Next, candidates change into a different set of white clothing. They carry a green apron embroidered with nine fig leaves, a cloth cap (with a veil attached for women), a white "robe" and a sashlike "girdle." They also wear special shoes. In the endowment room the candidate watches and takes part in a highly symbolic video. In the past, the scenes were enacted by live actors in various rooms. They hear a speech telling them that they have been washed clean of the blood of their generation, anointed in expectation of becoming kings and queens, priests and priestesses. They are told that each will be given a new name and a garment. They move behind a curtain where they hear various voices that are supposed to represent a conversation between Elohim, Jehovah and Michael. The creation scene is reenacted against a background made to look like the Garden of Eden. In a drama like one of the ancient mystery religions, the gods plan out the future of the first man, including a garden, the Tree of Knowledge of Good and Evil, the temptation by Lucifer and the law of sacrifice if he fails the test. Michael falls asleep and the endowees close their eyes as well. When they open them, Adam and Eve have appeared. The temptation of Adam and Eve is acted out. They eat the fruit so that they can replenish the earth (remember that in Mormonism the eating of the fruit is a good thing). Participants now put on the fig-leaf-covered apron. Endowees put on the new clothing as well. All swear to be willing to sacrifice their life and goods for the kingdom. They are taught the "First Token of the Aaronic Priesthood" which is a secret handshake. Up until 1990 they also promised that if they were to betray the secret, they would willingly pay for this betrayal by death.

Next, the participants observe Peter, James and John instructing Adam in "the Law of the Gospel," and are warned against light-mindedness, loud laughter, evil speaking of the Lord's anointed (the LDS prophet), and other immoral practices. Lucifer is cast out, but the inductees are warned that if they turn back from their covenant, they will be in his power. After other words and ceremonies, they now receive the Second Token of the Aaronic Priesthood, which is a different handshake from the first. Its sign is performed by bringing the right hand to the front with the hand cupped, the right hand forming a square and the left arm raised to the square. Before 1990, they agreed to give up their life rather than reveal the secret, at which point the worker symbolically made a cutting motion across their chest with the right hand (again, reminiscent of Masonic rites).

After other symbolic acts, the endowees view a video depicting the terrestrial world, make a vow to have sex only with their spouses, and are given the First Token of the Melchizedek Priesthood, also known as "the Sign of the Nail." This is still another intricate handshake with a motion symbolizing the piercing of the hand by a nail. Again, a hand motion involving a cupped hand and a square formed by the hands is performed.

Next, the participant is taught the Second Token of the Melchizedek Priesthood. They vow to keep the "Law of Consecration" which is in the *Doctrine and Covenants*. They vow to devote time, energy, talents and material possessions to the Church (knowing that their bishop back home will keep track of how well they fulfill this vow). They then exchange the "Patriarchal Grip," which is an even more complex hand motion representing the second nail that those who killed Jesus put through his wrist, in the "sure place."

Then, after prayers and other ceremonies, the endowees see a large curtain opened, behind which is wide archway, supported by five pillars. Between the pillars are embroidered veils with the same marks on them which will be embroidered on their undergarments for the rest of their lives—a compass (representing a course for eternal life), a square (representing the endowment oaths), a navel mark (symbolic of physical and spiritual health), and knee marks (representing bowing the knee to God). Endowees then demonstrate their knowledge of the secret handshakes by exchanging them through a hole in the embroidered veil with a worker behind the veil. They are also asked questions by a person behind the veil.

Other ritual ceremonies are performed at this time. Finally, the endowees pass through the veil where they are received in an elaborately furnished room representing the celestial kingdom. Those to be married immediately after their endowment proceed to have their eternal marriage "sealed." The sealing ceremony is done in a room with multiple mirrors. Before sealing the marriage they are asked to use the mirrors to contemplate their progression when they become gods.

We have already noticed the close parallel between the Mormon endowments and Masonic lodge ordinances. The square, compass, secret handshakes, oaths whispered through a veil, receiving of a secret name, and even the shoes and garments worn were co-opted directly from Masonic ceremonies. Joseph Smith claimed that he was reviving an inspired version of a corrupt ceremony the Masons had handed down from Solomon. More likely, Smith concluded that ritual ceremony would tie members more closely to him as their Prophet, and he simply adapted the ceremonies he had learned in Masonry for his own purposes.

## Baptism for the Dead

Those who have already gone through an endowment ceremony for themselves are eligible to go through vicarious baptism, better known to outsiders as baptism for the dead. Mormons are taught that they themselves cannot be exalted if they ignore their responsibility to research their genealogies and perform baptisms for their dead relatives. The Church maintains over 4500 "Family History Centers" in 70 countries to help Mormons to study their genealogies. In principle the family succession of baptized persons must form an unbroken chain back to Adam in order to assure participation in the highest level of the Celestial Kingdom.[110] Committed Mormons are often fascinated with, if not obsessed with genealogical studies. Anyone doing genealogy work will bump into Mormons at every turn.

Mormons are taught that proxy baptisms do not violate free will. In the spirit world, those for whom proxy baptism was performed will have the chance to accept salvation. If they do so, then their proxy baptism goes into effect. Mormons support their belief in salvation after death through proxy baptism by appealing to 1 Peter 3:18–19 and John 5:25–28. (Note: there is no mention of baptism or even salvation in these passages.) They justify baptism for the dead by a dubious use of 1 Corinthians 15:29 in which Paul refers *ad hoc* to people who are "baptized for the dead."[111]

Those to be baptized for the dead are asked the same qualifying questions they were asked before their endowment (see above). They are dressed in white baptism garments and led to a baptistery, always below ground level to emphasize the symbolism of *burial* in baptism. They then go through a scripted ceremony. Participants are told before each baptism, "I baptize you for and in behalf of Mary Jones" (for example). This process may be repeated multiple times, once for each person for whom the participant is being baptized on that day. After the baptisms, the one who has been baptized has hands laid on him/her—once for each of the people for whom he/she was baptized—in order that the dead person may receive the Holy Ghost.

Do Mormons really believe this works? Apparently so. Millions of deceased people have "received" proxy baptism carried out in their name. Clearly, this would be an offensive act to most non-Mormons.

It is certain that many of you reading this book have ancestors who have had a proxy baptism performed in their name. In 1995 the Mormon Church officially agreed to cease proxy baptisms for Jews, after loud public protests by various Jewish groups. A good personal friend who is now a Christian has shared with me that soon after her own baptism, she was baptized for thirteen other people.

## Mormon Lifestyle and Culture

All of us who know faithful Mormons personally have a similar testimony about our Mormon friends. By comparison to the world, and even by comparison to the majority of those who claim the name of Christian, our Mormon friends, on average, have closer families and live more outwardly moral lives. It is hard to fault Mormons or Mormonism for these admirable qualities. Studies by experts of measures such as divorce rate, church attendance, number of families with two parents, and so on support this conclusion. How does the church maintain this lifestyle? Might biblical Christians learn from them in these areas? It is time to try to answer this somewhat uncomfortable question.

Cause and effect may be difficult to establish, but a couple of factors suggest themselves. Why do Mormons, on average, have what appear to be stronger families even than their "Christian" counterparts? Their belief in celestial marriage and celestial families means eternity is at stake. Teaching, preaching, and programs geared to protecting and supporting families serve to emphasize the importance of family. Mormons are taught that divorce jeopardizes their place in the celestial kingdom. Of course, Jesus taught that God hates divorce, but Mormon teaching underscores Jesus' condemnation of divorce between believers.[112] Mormons are taught that the eternal destiny of their children and even of their ancestors can be affected by divorce. Because of the persecution which is part of their history, Mormons have tended to rely on themselves and to be isolated from their Gentile neighbors (us). This has caused them to focus on their families and their immediate church communities. Persecution has, paradoxically, strengthened Mormon families.

Can we learn from the families of our Mormon friends? The answer is yes, even though we reject their teaching about celestial marriage and proxy baptism. If we want stronger families, Christian churches must consistently emphasize the importance of family, the Christian prohibition of adultery and divorce, and we need teaching and programs that support strong families.

Before moving on, let us take a closer look at Mormon marriages. We should view what appears to be stronger marriages with some caution. Many who have looked closely at Mormon marriages have discovered a high rate of dissatisfaction—especially on the part of the wives. Marriage in Utah in the 1800s was not a positive experience for most of the women. Jon Krakauer, in his book *Under the Banner of Heaven*,[113] has written an exposé of the deep level of unhappiness of many Mormon wives today. They are barred from the priesthood and only gain entrance to the celestial kingdom through their husbands. The patriarchalism of Mormon culture has had a negative impact on Mormon wives and marriages.

And what about their seemingly better outward holiness? Mormons may have lower rates of sexual promiscuity, smoking, drug abuse and other sinful behaviors. It is difficult to deny that their church culture fosters an outwardly more moral lifestyle. If we recall the questions Mormons are asked on a regular basis before temple ceremonies (see above) we realize part of the explanation. Unless they are prepared to lie, Mormons know that they will be questioned and will have to answer to a religious leader who knows them personally—whether they have drunk alcohol or coffee, given a full 10% of their income, been sexually impure, and a number of other sensitive personal matters. Such semi-public accountability explains a good deal of Mormon morality.

What are we to make of this? Should we incorporate a similar kind of "discipling," one that involves regular, intrusive inquiries by church leaders of their members? Such actions might have some positive effect on outward actions; however, whether this would have an overall strong positive effect on the inward, spiritual life is a more dubious proposal. As Paul said to the Colossians about the creation of human rules,

> "Do not handle! Do not taste! Do not touch!" Such regulations indeed have an appearance of wisdom, with their self-imposed worship, their false humility and their harsh treatment of the body, but they lack any value in restraining sensual indulgence" (Colossians 2:23).

With this word of caution, we will concede that Mormons, on average, do maintain some Christian moral convictions at a high level, and we have no desire to disparage this. Instead, we Christians ought to appreciate what the Mormons have accomplished. Challenged, we ought to strive for a righteousness, so to speak, that exceeds that of the Pharisees (Matthew 5:20). We will return to the matter of our own Christian testimony and its role in outreach to Mormons in the next chapter.

## Can the LDS Church Become Christian?

A few more characteristics of Mormon life bear mention before we pass to our final chapter on helping our Mormon friends to become Christians. One thing to note is that the Utah Mormon group has moved slowly but steadily over the last fifty years away from the more radical Mormon teachings and toward mainstream Christianity. Should we think of this as a good thing? Might they evolve into a truly Christian church?

It is always a bad idea to criticize a person or a group for moving in the right direction, even if they are still far from the truth. Denouncing a Hindu, a Muslim, or a Mormon for giving to the poor or avoiding sexual immorality is unlikely to win him or her over to biblical Christianity. Besides, Mormons no longer practice or teach plural marriage or blood atonement. They no longer publicly teach and support the destruction of the United States government. Their endowment ceremonies no longer include oaths to cut out the tongues of those unfaithful to their endowments.[114] Mormons now accept non-whites into their priesthoods and have removed some of the most offensive wording about "dark and loathsome" people in their scripture. Some of the bizarre teachings, like the claim that Jesus was a polygamist, or that Adam is God the Father, are no longer taught or are so deemphasized that, for all practical purposes, we can assume most Mormons no longer believe them.

Returning to the question whether it is possible that Mormons might evolve into Christians, our answer is a strong *no*. Mormon teaching and practice predictably will continue to evolve in a direction which will allow it to be perceived as more mainstream. However, there are idiosyncratic aspects of Mormonism that cannot be abandoned if the church is to remain "Mormon." As long as the Mormon Church continues in their testimony that Joseph Smith is a prophet and the Book of Mormon is the Word of God, they will not be genuinely Christian. To accept that the Book of Mormon is the Word of God is to accept teaching that cannot be made compatible with the Bible. Even more significantly, to accept that Joseph Smith is a prophet is to accept his teaching of eternal progression and three different kingdoms. As Mormons have evolved, they have not moved away from this and other teaching spelled out clearly in *Doctrines and*

*Covenants*. The evolution of the Latter-day Saints has been principally in the temple ceremony and in the doctrines that are not clearly laid out in the *Doctrine and Covenants*. We predict that this pattern will continue because to do otherwise is to jeopardize the testimony that is the heart of Mormon belief. No, Mormonism will not evolve into biblical Christianity in the foreseeable future.

## Other Mormon Groups

There are a number of sects that have broken away from the mainline of Mormonism, and knowing something about their existence is important if we are to avoid the error of viewing Mormonism as a monolithic and unified entity.

## Community of Christ

We have already described the history of the formation of the Reformed Church of Jesus Christ of Latter-day Saints (RLDS). In 2001 this group formally changed its name to the Community of Christ. It is difficult to judge motives, but we can speculate that they have chosen to move away from the LDS label, as it raises red flags for many. Besides, having the word "Reformed" in their name was awkward. To many non-members this group is informally known as the "Missouri Mormons," to distinguish them from the "Utah Mormons."

This group had its genesis in a "reorganization" of the Mormon Church in April, 1860. The impetus for this move came from William Smith, the only surviving sibling of Joseph Smith Jr. William and his nephew Joseph Smith III had briefly aligned themselves with the Strangite group, but when James Strang declared openly for polygamy, William left this breakaway group and began to organize his own sect of Mormonism. Joseph Smith III was appointed the President and Prophet of the RLDS in 1860, at which time the church was officially organized. Part of the justification for forming this sect was the fact, verified even by many in the Utah LDS, that Joseph, Jr. had designated his son Joseph III as his successor. The RLDS was formally headed by a direct descendant of Joseph Smith until the death of Wallace B. Smith in 1996. The RLDS accepted much of the doctrine we associated with the LDS, as described in the previous chapter, but Joseph Smith III turned away from the teaching of polygamy and blood atonement. The strongest driving force behind the formation of the RLDS, besides their rejection of the teaching of polygamy was their rejection of the leadership of Brigham Young. William called him a "Pontius Pilate and a "Nero." They labeled Young a false prophet and blamed him for inventing the doctrine of polygamy and for deceitfully claiming Smith supported polygamy in order to legitimize the doctrine. History does not agree with the RLDS interpretation of the source of this doctrine. There is more than adequate evidence that Joseph Smith Jr. both taught and practiced polygamy.

The official list of scripture of the Community of Christ includes their own edition of the *Book of Mormon*, the *Doctrine and Covenants* (minus the revelation of Brigham Young and the 1890 and 1978 additions), as well as Joseph Smith's "Inspired Version" of the Bible. They do not include the *Book of Abraham* but do accept the *Book of Moses*. The group owns the original temple at Kirtland, operating it as a historical site. They opened a temple in Independence, Missouri in 1994. The group claims 250,000 members worldwide. They comprise roughly two percent of those who claim Joseph Smith as a prophet.

We can see the RLDS as a more moderate form of Mormonism. They have made a conscious effort to more toward the mainstream of Christianity. They describe themselves as a "Restorationist Movement," trying to put themselves in the same camp as the Christian Church and the Churches of Christ. Whether they will succeed in this attempt is doubtful. Their doctrine of eternal progression is more moderate than that of the LDS. Because they accept the *Doctrine and Covenants*, they cannot completely turn away from the idea of progression but they deny that those in the celestial kingdom achieve the status of godhood. I have stated my belief above that Mormons will not be able to successfully complete a move into the mainstream of Christianity and remain Mormon in any real sense. The Community of Christ is a test case. The problem for this group is that as long as they include the *Doctrine and Covenants*, the Book of Mormon and the Joseph Smith Version of the Bible in their canon, they will not be accepted by most groups as fully Christian.

## Fundamentalist Latter-day Saints

On the other extreme of the LDS from the Community of Christ is the range of groups which are described as Fundamentalist Latter-day Saints (FLDS). There is a confusing array of groups which can be placed into the category of fundamentalist Mormons. The distinguishing characteristic of these groups is that they continue to both teach and practice polygamy. The largest defined groups of fundamentalist Mormons are the Apostolic United Brethren, headed by J. LaMoine Jenson, and the FLDS. The Jenson group are centered in a region south of Salt Lake City and have about 7000 members. More well-known to the American public is the group which carries the name Fundamentalist Latter-day Saints (FLDS). They are headed by members of the Jeffs clan and are centered around the Utah/Arizona border, with about 8000 members. An enclave of the FLDS in Eldorado Texas was the subject of a raid which received worldwide media attention. Dozens of children were removed from their extended families under suspicion of polygamy and forced marriage of minors. There are many other splinter groups scattered in the United States, Mexico and Canada. A recent Reuters article (2007)[115] estimated a total of 40,000 who could be described as fundamentalist Mormons.

A number of exposes of the fundamentalist Mormon movement have been published recently. One of these is *The Nineteenth Wife,* by David Ebershoff.[116] It is a fictionalized account of the nineteen wife of Brigham Young that is used by the author as an opportunity to critique the practices of current-day fundamentalist Mormon groups which continue the legacy of Brigham Young. Another is *Under the Banner of Heaven: A Story of Violent Faith,* by Jon Krakauer.[117] This is a chilling nonfiction account of the murder of a mother and her daughter for refusing to accept being forced into a plural marriage. The book is more than an account of the murder. It gives a good summary of the various fundamentalist groups and what drives people to join these groups. The fundamentalist Mormons are highly patriarchal. Many live in compounds, almost completely isolated from the world, ruled over by male leaders with an iron hand. Young men who are not sufficiently spiritual to be given wives are often expelled from the groups, allowing the inner, privileged few men to take multiple wives.

However, not all those who can be described as fundamentalist Mormons live in such isolated compounds. Many live in normal neighborhoods, especially in Utah and Arizona. They live a "double" life, working in regular jobs during the day, but keeping multiple wives in secret.

The fundamentalist Mormons argue, not without merit, that they represent the true legacy of Joseph Smith. It would be even more accurate to describe them as maintaining the true legacy of Brigham Young.

## Should I vote for a Mormon?

As I write this, the presumptive candidate for the Republican nomination to the presidency of the United States is a Mormon. Most of those reading this book will know the result of this election. Should a Christian be willing to vote for a Mormon? Those who do not live in the United States may never face this dilemma. It certainly is not my place to tell anyone how they should vote. Still, one might ask, "Could anyone who accepts the seemingly irrational claims of Joseph Smith and the Book of Mormon be a good president, where the ability to think rationally is a requirement?" This seems a legitimate question.

Political ideology aside, many Mormons have served admirably in the United States Government. Harry Reid is the current United States Senate Majority Leader and is a Democrat. Orrin Hatch is one of the most powerful and respected US Senators and is a Republican. Brent Scowcroft served admirably under Gerald Ford and George H. W. Bush as the head of National Security. Mormon politicians have tended to be moderate in their leanings. Bill Marriott is the Chairman and CEO of one of the most respected corporations in the world. It is a little-known fact that the CIA has gone out of its way to recruit Mormons in their organization. Why is that? The reason is that those raised in Mormon communities share a few qualities valuable to the intelligence industry. Mormons have learned to be discreet. We will discuss their policy of "milk before meat" below. Mormons are trained early to answer questions carefully. They are willing to hold back certain kinds of information in order to affect the thinking of those with whom they speak (Gentiles). Another common characteristic of Mormons is that they are scrupulously honest in their dealings with one another and with outsiders. They are extremely difficult to corrupt. It is not without reason that the Latter-day Saints have a reputation for hard work. Mormons accept a view of the history of the Americas which cannot be supported by evidence. We might conclude that they are easily duped and not well educated. This is not the case. As a whole, Mormons have traditionally strongly supported education. A disproportionate number of Mormons complete a college education and pursue professional careers.

Should a Christian be willing to vote for a Mormon? The qualities described are ones which are excellent qualifications for a leader of any political stripe. Who a Christian ought to vote for is a matter of personal choice, but being a Mormon does not disqualify a person from public office. We could even argue that, to the extent such stereotypes apply, it is a net positive.

# Chapter 9

# Sharing the Gospel with Mormons

For most of those reading this book, their principle interest is not in finding the "dirt" on Mormonism. Their desire is to help Mormons make the transition to a more biblical form of Christianity. Most are aware that Mormons are extremely difficult to "convert." The purpose of this chapter is to provide some guidance to aid those trying to reach out to their Mormon friends with the gospel.

## Why Is It So Hard to Convert Mormons?

Let us first be reminded of a few things we already know about Mormons that explains why they are difficult to proselytize. First of all, we need to bear in mind the central fact that their belief is based principally on emotion, not on rational knowledge. It is supported by a carefully guarded "testimony," rather than by logical argument or factual information. When faced with what would appear to be a logical or factual inconsistency in Mormon teaching or in their scripture, the typical response of a follower of Joseph Smith is not to produce a counterargument. The Mormon response to most argument is, "All I know is that Joseph Smith is a prophet and the Book of Mormon is the Word of God." It is extremely unlikely that we will be able to "argue" our Mormon friends into becoming a biblical Christian. Most attempts to do so are counterproductive.

The fundamental role of testimony in Mormonism is illustrated by *D&C* 9:8–9. "But, behold, I say unto you, that you must study it out in your mind; then you must ask me if it be right, and if it is right I will cause that your bosom shall burn within you; therefore, you shall feel that it is right. But if it be not right you shall have no such feelings, but you shall have a stupor of thought that shall cause you to forget the thing which is wrong." Here Joseph is speaking to Oliver Cowdery. Mormons worldwide has used the same means to prop up their faith. The "evidence" of Mormonism is not historical fact or fulfilled prophecy, it is a burning within. Once a Mormon has this religious experience, it is difficult to disprove such an experience. Mormon apologist D. Michael Quinn said about the authority of religious experience:

> In spiritual knowledge, I must say that my own experiences with prayer, the Spirit and revelation are primary evidence, whereas the evidence and testimony of the scriptures, of the prophets and other good, believing people and of the historical record of mankind are secondary.[118]

In "Teachings of the Living Prophets"—a manual used in classes at BYU, the following quote appeared: "We rely therefore on the teachings of the living oracles of God as of equal validity with the doctrines of the written word.[119]

There is another quality shared by most Mormons that limits their "openness" to considering other Christian groups. They sincerely believe that they are more "Christian" than any other group that claims the name. This contributes to their conviction that they are the reestablished Christian Church and are the only group eligible for the celestial kingdom. This belief is regularly reinforced by the behavior exhibited by many who profess the name Christian. We made the case in the previous chapter that, if viewed from the outward manifestation of Christian morality, this Mormon stereotype is often confirmed. The high divorce rate, acceptance of premarital sex, problems with drinking and other kinds of hypocrisy in the lives of "Gentiles" who call themselves Christians reinforces the stereotypes Mormons have about those they believe are not legitimate Saints. A devoted follower of Christ wants to argue that if we exclude nominal Christians (those who take the name Christian but who have not made a comprehensive decision to live like Christ) the equation will change significantly. This may not be an effective argument because our Mormon friends have been taught from their youth that *all* of us are nominal Christians.

Another reason it can be extremely difficult to help Mormons toward a more biblical form of Christianity is an emotional one. Those raised within Mormonism have been taught to believe that if they are sealed in a temple and later leave the Mormon faith their final place will be in the lowest hell. They become the lowest of the low. This teaching was one reason the blood atonement doctrine took hold (although it has been repudiated by all Mormons today). Latayne Scott described the feelings that came to her mind as she considered leaving:

> But for a Mormon, you're either in or out. You're either a child, a potential Mormon Gentile, a post-baptism "confirmed" Mormon, or a member of a third class too horrible to contemplate. Consciously and permanently leaving the Mormon Church takes one beyond any hope. Apostasy from Mormonism—the idea of becoming what is called a son of perdition—is that of the sealed fate of a creature past redemption, a being of utter loss, beyond any spiritual lifeline or resuscitation, dead to God yet still living, a walking corpse.[120]

Mormons live within a very tight community. Their isolation from Gentiles, sustained by persecution, heightens their sense of community. Add to this the teaching about celestial families. To leave the family's commitment to the LDS church is not only to lose one's place in the celestial kingdom. Mormons believe that it also affects the place of other family members. It is a common experience of Mormon couples that if one spouse repudiates Joseph Smith, the other will be advised to divorce the one who left the church. I studied the Bible with a friend in just this situation. When he left his faith, his wife left him, took their four children to Utah and filed for divorce. She was advised to do this by her bishop. We will see from testimonies below that those who leave their family commitment to the Mormon faith go through a process akin to divorce or even the death of a loved one. Author Latayne Scott went through this separation from her Mormon family. She said, "For a faithful Mormon, leaving this way of life is as hard as trying to accustom oneself to life in a foreign country."[121] We should not minimize how difficult it is for people to put away their LDS testimony.

## What Should I Do?

How is a Christian to deal with these seemingly insurmountable barriers to reaching out to Mormons? First of all, let us realize that this will not be easy. Here are a few suggestions:

## Do not argue with Mormons

It was Jonathan Swift (author of Gulliver's Travels) who said, "You cannot reason someone out of something they were not reasoned into in the first place." Because the Mormon testimony is based on a "burning in the heart," rather than evidence or reasoning, presenting logical answers to our Mormon friends, alone, will not generally be sufficient. A personal testimony from a friend will illustrate this point.

Joe Fields, author of the original summary of the Book of Mormon adapted in this book, shares a story of a Mormon whom he helped to become a Christian: Several years ago a missionary came to his door in Tucson, Arizona. Joe agreed to study with the "elder" if he would agree to give equal time to a study of the Bible with Joe. After a five-hour presentation from the missionary over two sessions, Joe went over the study on covenants presented below. The man left with no evidence that the study of covenants had had any effect on his testimony. One year later, finished with his mission, the man called Joe. "The study really shook me up," he said. They met in a neutral site, began to study the scriptures and the former missionary became a Christian. The idea of covenant had really worked for him. It was like a "sugar stick" (Joe's words), as covenant is such a big concept in Mormonism. The effect was not a sudden one. He did not lose his testimony right away, but over several months, the idea of covenants did not go away. Gradually, his faith in the Book of Mormon decreased until one day he found his testimony had been lost.

Why had it been so hard for him to contemplate leaving the LDS? The man shared that what made it hard for him to leave was the incredible support system within Mormonism. If he had left during his mission, he would have completely lost his support. Even when he finished his mission, the support system continued. He was given a loan at nearly 0% to start a business. The Mormons take care of their own, but those who leave lose this support.

This testimony raises some helpful points for us. First, a perfectly rational argument alone cannot defeat the testimony of most Mormons; or if it can, the effect is not immediate. The inconsistency in the Book of Mormon with regard to covenants could not, by itself, destroy the faith of this missionary. Joe was able to present a seed of doubt, but such seeds need time to grow.

Another point we can glean from this testimony is that the "conversion" of a Mormon normally occurs in two discrete stages:

1. The Mormon loses his or her testimony.

2. (later) The Mormon comes to believe in Christ.

In the testimony above, it took several months for the missionary to lose his faith in Joseph Smith and his book. Only after he lost his testimony was he open to studying the gospel and becoming a Christian.

A side note: The previous testimony might be thought of as an encouragement to use the visit of a Mormon elder/missionary to one's door as a chance to convert him or at least to get him to doubt his testimony. I advise that you do not attempt to "convert" a Mormon missionary when he comes to your door. They are not there to learn from you. Experts in Mormonism agree that the likelihood of "converting" a Mormon missionary is near zero. Even if you are able to plant a seed of doubt in the elder who comes to your door, if the missionary begins to question his testimony, he will be immediately sent to another mission station. There is nothing wrong with politely turning down the missionary's request to talk. If you want to take the time to plant a seed (see below), it is advised to make a single simple point and, no matter what, do not engage in arguments.

What I have observed from talking to several former Mormons agrees with the testimony of experts whose ministry is reaching out to them. LDS members must first lose their testimony and apostatize from Mormonism before they can be converted to Christ. The time span between the two stages will vary greatly, but the process seems to be consistent.

Another testimony illustrates the fact that leaving Mormonism and becoming a Christian are not simultaneous events:

A woman from Utah does not want to be identified. Some of her family members are still in the LDS, and even now, over thirty years after she left the church, to bring up the circumstances of her leaving would be to open a large and unhealed would. This is a common theme in Mormon conversions. She grew up as a good Mormon girl in a good Mormon family. As with most Mormons, she was part of a very caring but closed community. She was raised to assume that she would always be a Mormon. In high school she attended the churches of some of her friends occasionally. Looking back now, she remembers one thing that really stuck out to her, which is that in her LDS church Jesus was rarely even mentioned. She heard a lot about Joseph Smith and the inspiring stories of the Utah pioneers. As she progressed in her Mormon testimony, her religious life became mostly a matter of "legalistically" following rules such as the Word of Wisdom and performing ceremonies that had little meaning for her spiritually. Her testimony was weakened over time, but it was a catastrophic event that caused her to lose her faith. As she had been told to expect, she married a "good" LDS boy and prepared to settle into her family, preparing for life in the celestial kingdom together. Then her "good" Mormon husband abandoned her and the children. Her faith in the hope of joy in this life was destroyed. Even after her testimony was shattered, to leave the church was "like an angry divorce." She hated Mormonism, but she still loved it, including the community that had given her such security growing up.

Ultimately she left the church. She became "almost an agnostic." She wanted nothing to do with religion. This is an oft-repeated pattern. Those who leave Mormonism are usually left with nothing. To lose their faith in Joseph Smith is to lose faith entirely. She remained an unbeliever for many years. It was only several years later, after marrying a man who truly loved her and who had faith in Christ that she was able to hear the gospel message. She is a happy and well-adjusted Christian today.

If helping a Mormon is a two-step process (first a person must take an emotional step away from Mormonism, then, only later, can he or she be brought to Christ), what can we do to help an LDS person to make the first step? Consider three suggestions:

## 1. Plant a seed

Arguing with Mormons will not help. However, we can present to our Latter-day Saint friends a simple argument and allow that to be a seed. Latayne Scott, author of *The Mormon Mirage*, has gathered dozens of testimonies of former Mormons who later became disciples of Jesus. In many but not all of these cases, the seed was planted by a Christian (in other cases the seed was bad behavior by a fellow Mormon). Scott calls these seeds "points of departure." The only pattern she observed in these points of departure is that there was no pattern. She lists the following real examples: "a book left on a desk by a coworker, observing Mormon friends brawl, a pamphlet long forgotten in a pocket, an invitation to a Bible Study, A Christian tract in the mail, a "burning in the bosom" while attending a Protestant church, reading an early edition of *Doctrine and Covenants*, noticing that Joseph Smith had mislabeled as a man a woman [in one of the facsimiles in the *Book of Abraham*]. An informal poll was done through a website for former Mormons, asking why they left. Two-thirds of those who responded said that it was when they learned about Mormon history. Others said that they disagreed with leaders' ethics. Those who questioned the ethics of the Mormon hierarchy specially mentioned leaders such as Gordon B. Hinkley, who lied in a live interview about Church teaching on polygamy and godhood.[122]

A friend in my local church left Mormonism more than thirty years ago. He became a Christian a little over a year ago. He shares that the seed which caused him to lose his testimony was planted when he was in high school. He lived next door to the bishop of his local branch. His best friend was the child of the bishop. It was the hypocrisy he saw in the everyday life of the dysfunctional family of his bishop which, years later, corroded his testimony.

## 2. Watch your personal testimony

Mormons are taught that those who progress in their spiritual journey through participation in Mormon covenant activities are happier, better adjusted, have better families and live more moral, "Christian" lives. If we want to help our LDS friends to be open to a valid form of Christianity, then we must be careful about our personal testimony. To the extent it is within our power, we need to prove the stereotype that Mormons are more "Christian" to be a false one. Every time a person who claims to be a Christian slams the door angrily in the face of a Mormon missionary, they add confirmation to the Mormon perception that other Christian groups are not the real deal—that we are angry and unloving.

How is your testimony? Is your relationship with God strong? Is it obvious to those around you that you are more joyful and at peace than the crowd? Do you behave at work with absolute honesty? Are you a Daniel (Daniel 6:4–5)? Is helping the poor and needy a regular part of your life? Do you practice biblical purity? What is the strength of your Christian relationships? If you are married, and if you have a family, can anyone who visits your home tell that God is king of your home and that your family is different because of Christ in your life? Jesus told his followers, "You are the light of the world," and "let your light shine before men, so that they can see your good works, and give glory to your Father in heaven" (Matthew 5:15–16). This commandment is of particular importance in order to help Mormons come to Christ. Why? It is because their faith is based, not on rational evidence, but on testimony. If you want to help a Mormon, share about your Christian marriage and how God has changed your life. Such testimony may not have an immediate effect, but it might become an element in planting the seed that helps a Mormon to escape from his or her false theology.

### 3. Pray

Does it need to be said? If you have a friend, a relative, or a coworker who is a member of the LDS Church, you should pray for that person. Now that you have more information on the history and beliefs of Mormonism, your prayers can be more specific. You can pray that God can use you to plant a seed. You can ask God to help your friend to see the inconsistencies in Mormon history. You can pray for God to help you to let your testimony shine in a way that will change the heart. As Paul said, "I planted the seed, Apollos watered it, but God made it grow" (1 Corinthians 3:6). We can and should plant seeds. We can water those seeds by loving and listening to our Mormon friends. But God must make the seed grow.

## Practical Advice for Studying with Mormons or Former Mormons

Those who have studied the Bible with current or former members of the Latter-day Saints have some practical advice to bear in mind. First, we need to be "as shrewd as snakes and as innocent as doves" (Matthew10:16). Our Mormon friends have been trained carefully to not be completely honest about what they believe. Talking to a Mormon may make one feel like a reporter for the media interviewing a politician. "Can't they just give a straight answer to the question?" Mormons have a name for this approach to answering our questions. They call it "milk before meat."

It was mentioned above that on national media LDS President Gordon B. Hinkley lied about his beliefs. During his presidency, which began in 1995, he offered interviews to *Sixty Minutes*, *Larry King Live* and *Time*. In these interviews he refused to admit or even flatly denied that the Mormon Church teaches that God was once a man or that faithful Mormons expect to become a god one day. Quotes from speeches by Hinkley to his followers show that he lied. Your Mormon friend will most likely not flat-out lie about what he or she believes. The Mormon believer has been trained to change the subject from "meat" (in other words from touchy subjects) to "milk" (i.e., non-controversial things which most Christians would, in principle, agree with). If you are having a discussion (remember: not an argument!) with a Mormon or a former Mormon, you should be patient, loving, yet firm. Be aware that they are most likely going to steer away from answering questions that might prove problematic.

For example, a good question to ask a Mormon is whether he or she believes the Bible is without error—the inspired word of God. The answer may be evasive because LDS members are taught that the Catholic Church changed the Bible. You can ask whether your friend believes that the Bible has been changed, and if so, when and by whom? What is the evidence for this?[123] It is good to lay solid groundwork for future questions by getting the one you are studying with to commit on specific questions. Another good question to ask is whether he or she believes that the Book of Mormon and the *Doctrine and Covenants* is without error and inspired by God. This will be easier for a Mormon to answer, but you might want to ask some more pointed questions on what is meant by the answer. For example, you can ask if it would ever be needful to change the perfect inspired scripture for any reason. Remember that the LDS church teaches continued revelation. They also have not hesitated to change the wording in the supposedly inspired Book of Mormon if it served their purposes.[124]

Another factor to bear in mind is that your LDS friend will probably insist on using the King James Version of the Bible. Mormons do this because they have been trained to use this version only. This is because some of the wording in this version parallels their way of explaining their faith (for example their use of the term Holy Ghost rather than Holy Spirit), and because the Book of Mormon uses wording, supposedly inspired, which is an exact replication of parts of the King James Bible. You may prefer to use another version. However, it is advisable to let your friend use the King James

Version. You may agree to do all your studying in this version, or at the least to let your friend use his or her KJV and for you to use the version you are comfortable with.

Another suggestion when you study with a Mormon is to get on the table as soon as possible a clear understanding about the authority of the Bible which both of you agree on. You should also get established as clearly as possible their view of the authority and reliability of the Book of Mormon, *D&C* and the *Pearl.*

In closing, we want to share a study of covenants in the Bible and in the Book of Mormon which has been used with success to help Mormons leave their faith in Joseph Smith and the Book of Mormon. It has been adapted from a study developed by Joe Fields.[125] The study was created on the premise that it is wise to study the Bible and the Book of Mormon in an area where we have common ground. The common ground in this case is in the doctrine of covenants. If you want to plant a seed with your Mormon friend, you should not do a study on the character of Joseph Smith or Brigham Young. Having a study in the *Doctrine and Covenants* about plural marriage and contrasting that with the Bible will not be useful.

To the Mormon, the idea of covenant is like meat and potatoes. It is like bread and butter. The typical Mormon has heard dozens of sermons and lessons on the idea of the covenant and on the revival of the covenant by Joseph Smith in 1830. As you prepare to use this study, the words in italics below are intended to explain to you the purpose and the answer you should expect to receive from a Mormon. To do this study, you will need a Book of Mormon, a King James Version of the Bible, and possibly another version of the Bible you are more comfortable with. The study can be done in two or more parts. The purpose of this study is to establish that if we believe in the idea of a covenant between man and God, we must either reject the Bible or the Book of Mormon. Their understanding of covenant is irreconcilable.

# The Word of God

What books are identified as the words of God? 2 Nephi 29:13

> "...words of the Jews" The Bible
> " words of the lost tribes of Israel" Lost books?
> "...words of the Nephites" Book of Mormon

*Here we are establishing that the Mormons believe that the Bible and the Book of Mormon are equally the inspired Word of God, and that the Book of Mormon anticipates other inspired scriptures.*

What does "...they both shall be established in one" mean? 1 Nephi 13:41
*Further establishing that the BOM and the Bible are of equal authority.*

What are the "plain and precious things" that were taken from the Bible? 1 Nephi 13:28

*Here we are airing the Mormon belief that the Bible has been changed. You may want to explore the specifics and the evidence they use to support these specifics.*

Do the Bible and the Book of Mormon have to be in harmony with each other?

*Hopefully the answer will be yes.*

What are the two sticks in Ezekiel 37:15–22?

*Mormons are taught (wrongly) that this is a biblical prophecy of the Bible and the Book of Mormon.*

What version of the Bible do you accept as the inspired word of God?

*This is important, as Mormons will normally commit to the King James Version to be inspired and authoritative.*

Does God's word in the Book of Mormon ever contradict God's word in the Bible?

Would there ever be any reason to reject the Bible as God's word?

*Here we are getting into the meat of the study. The point to be established is that in the Bible there is no confusion between foreshadow (in the Old Testament) and fulfillment of the foreshadow (in the New Testament) whereas in the BOM, the fulfillment occurs before the foreshadow.*

# Infinite and Eternal Atonement

**Alma 34:14 / Hebrews 10:1**

| Atonement Foreshadow | Atonement Applied |
|---|---|
| Book of Mormon | Book of Mormon |
| Mosiah 16:14 (148 BC) | Mosiah 4:2,3 (124 BC) |
| 2 Nephi 25:24–27 (545 BC) | Jacob 4:11 (421 BC) |
| Alma 33:19–22 (74 BC) | Jarom 1:11 (399 BC) |
| Mosiah 12:31–13:28 (148 BC) | Alma 7:14 (83 BC) |
| Alma 25:15 (77 BC) | |
| | |
| The Old Testament | The New Testament |
| Genesis 12:3 (1500 BC) | Galatians 3:8 (AD 49) |
| Numbers 21:4-9 (1500 BC) | John 3:14, 12:32 (AD 85–90) |
| Isaiah 53:4-7 (701 BC) | 1 Peter 2:21-25 (AD 64) |
| Exodus 12:1 (1500 BC) | 1 Corinthians 5:7 (AD 54) |
| Leviticus 4 (1500 BC) | Hebrews 9 (AD 60–69) |
| | |
| (Hebrews 10:1, Galatians 3:24) | (Galatians 3:19,23, Colossians 2:14) |

# The Mystery

**Ephesians 1:8–10: (NIV2011)**

"With all wisdom and understanding, he made known to us the *mystery* of his will according to his good pleasure, which he purposed in Christ, to be put into effect when the times reach their fulfillment—to bring unity to all things in heaven and on earth under Christ.

**Ephesians 3:3–5 (NIV2011)**

That is, the *mystery* made known to me by revelation, as I have already written briefly. In reading this, then, you will be able to understand my insight into the mystery of Christ, which was not made known to people in other generations as it has now been revealed by the Spirit to God's holy apostles and prophets.

**Ephesians 3:6 (NIV2011)**

This *mystery* is that through the gospel the Gentiles are heirs together with Israel, members together of one body, and sharers together in the promise in Christ Jesus.

**Ephesians 3:8–9 (NIV2011)**

Although I am less than the least of all the Lord's people, this grace was given me: to preach to the Gentiles the boundless riches of Christ, and to make plain to everyone the administration of this *mystery*, which for ages past was kept hidden in God, who created all things.

# The Plan of Redemption

*Atonement in Christ before the foundation of the world*

| Law of Moses | 1500–400 BC | New Testament |
|---|---|---|
| Leviticus 16 | Animal Sacrifices | Hebrews 9:11–14 |
| Exodus 20:8 | Keep the Sabbath | Colossians 2:14–16 |
| **Book of Mormon** | | |
| Jarom 1:5,11 | Law of Moses / Sabbath | 399 BC |
| 2 Nephi 25:24–27 | Belief in Christ | 545 BC |
| Jn 3:16 | Belief | |
| Mosiah 4:2 | Atonement Applied | 124 BC |
| Rom 3:25 | Atonement | |
| Alma 7:14 | Baptism for Remission of Sin | 83 BC |
| Acts 2:38 | Baptism | |
| Alma 46:15 | Called Christian | 73 BC |
| Acts 11:26 | Christian | |

What arrangement did God make for atonement under the Law of Moses?
What did the Nephites command in regard to atonement?
What event fulfilled the Law of Moses?

| The Patriarchs | Law of Moses | New Testament |
|---|---|---|
| Adam / Eve | Ex 20 Ten Commandments | 2 Co 3:6 Spirit of Law |
| Cain / Abel | Nu 3:10 Temple/Priesthood | 2 Pet 2:5 All Believers |
| Noah / Ark | Animal sacrifices | Heb 10:8–10 Crucifixion |

Were those under the Law of Moses required to build an ark? Yes / No

Was Noah required to offer animal sacrifice for sin? Yes / No

Are Christians required to keep the Law of Moses? Yes / No

Were those under the Law of Moses required to accept the atonement of Christ? Yes / No

# End Notes

1. Joseph Fielding Smith, *Doctrines of Salvation* (Salt Lake City: Bookcraft, 1954–56), 1:188.

2. Douglas Jacoby has additional material on Mormonism in a podcast available at http://www.jacobypremium.com/images/podcasts/CE408-Mormon.mp3.

3. Although many sources are used in this history of Joseph Smith, the author would like to acknowledge that the principle source used in the first four chapters is the definitive book on the life of Joseph Smith, *No One Knows My Story*, by Fawn M. Brodie (New York: Vintage Books, 1995).

4. Lucy Smith, *Biographical Sketches of Joseph Smith the Prophet and His Progenitors for Many Generations* (Liverpool, England, 1853), 85.

5. *Latter Day Saints Messenger and Advocate*, Vol. 1 (Kirtland, Ohio, Nov. 6, 1834).

6. Joseph Smith, *History of the Church of Jesus Christ of Latter-Day Saints*, Vol. 1 (Salt Lake City: Deseret News, 1902), Vol. 1, 5–7. (From here on, we will refer to these volumes as simply *History of the Church.*)

7. Lucy Mack Smith, *Biographical Sketches of Joseph Smith the Prophet and His Progenitors for Many Generations* (Liverpool, Reformed Church of Jesus Christ of Latter-day Saints, 1853), 91–92.

8. Adapted from Fawn M. Brodie, *No Man Knows My Story* (New York: Vintage Books, 1995), 432. Originally in Eber D. Howe, *Mormonism Unvailed* (sic) (Painesville, Ohio: Published by author, 1843).

9. Joseph Smith, *History of the Church*, Vol. 1, p. 220.

10. Jonathan Edwards went so far as to produce a tract in which he claimed to find close parallels between one of the native languages, that of the Muhhekaneew, and ancient Hebrew.

11. *Saints Herald*, Vol. XXVI (October 1, 1879), 289.

12. David Whitmer, *An Address to All Believers in Christ* (Richmond, Missouri, 1887).

13. Taken from Anthon's letter to E. D. Howe, dated February 17, 1834, in *Mormonism Unvailed* (sic), 270–272.

14. Lucy Smith, *Biographical Sketches of Joseph Smith the Prophet and His Progenitors for Many Generations* (Liverpool: Reorganized Church of Jesus Christ of Latter-day Saints, 1853), 121.

15. Joseph Smith, *Doctrine and Covenants*, Section 17.

16. Joseph Smith, *History of the Church of Jesus Christ of Latter-day Saints*, Vol.1 (Lamoni, Iowa: Reorganized Church of Jesus Christ of Latter-day Saints, 1897), 54–55.

17. Related by J. A. Clark, from *Gleanings by the Way* (Philadelphia: W.J. and J. K. Simmon, 1842), 256–257.

18. Joseph Smith, *Doctrine and Covenants*, 3:12 and 10:7.

19. Joseph Smith, *A Book of Commandments for the Government of the Church of Christ, Organized According to the Law, on the 6th of April, 1830* (Independence, Missouri: W. W. Phelps and Co., 1933), ch 16, 41.

20. Page's seer stone is in a collection of the Reorganized Church of Latter-day Saints, Independence, Missouri.

21. Joseph Smith, *Doctrine and Covenants*, Section 28.

22. Joseph seemed to confuse dreams and visions, even in his book. In the Book of Mormon, Lehi says, "Behold, I have dreamed a dream; or, in other words, I have seen a vision" (1 Nephi 8:2).

23. Fawn M. Brodie, *No Man Knows My History* (New York: Random House, 1995), 85.

24. *Doctrine and Covenants*, Section 28.

25. The Stone-Campbell Movement evolved into what is known as the Restoration Movement. The Churches of Christ and the Christian Church are the principle inheritors of this movement today.

26. Thomas B. Marsh, one of the quorum of the Twelve said of a speech given by Smith in October 1838, during the Mormon War, "I have heard the Prophet say that he would yet tread down his enemies, and walk over their dead bodies; and if he was not let alone, he would be a second Mohammad to this generation, and that he would make it one gore of blood from the Rocky Mountains to the Atlantic Ocean; that like Mohammad, whose motto in treating for peace was, 'the Alcoran or the Sword.' So should it be eventually with us, 'Joseph Smith or the Sword'" *History of the Church*, 3:167.

27. A brief sampling from Campbell's arguments: Passing over a hundred similar errors, we shall notice his ignorance of the New Testament matters and things. The twelve Apostles of the Lamb, are said by Paul, to have developed certain secrets, which were hid for ages and generations, which Paul says were ordained before the world to their glory, that they should have the honor of announcing them. But Smith makes his pious hero Nephi, 600 years before the Messiah began to preach, and disclose these secrets concerning the calling of the Gentiles, and the blessings flowing through the Messiah to Jews and Gentiles, which Paul says were hid for ages and generations, 'which in these ages was not made known unto the sons of men, as it is now revealed unto us the holy Apostles and prophets, by the spirit; that the Gentiles should be fellow heirs and of the same body and partakers of his promise in Christ by the Gospel [Romans 16:25–26].' Smith makes Nephi express every truth found in the writings of the Apostles concerning the calling and blessing of the Gentiles, and even quotes the 11th chapter of Romans, and many other passages before he had a son grown in the wilderness able to aim an arrow at a deer. Paul says these things were secrets and unknown until his time; but Smith makes Nephi say the same things 600 years before Paul was converted! One of the two is a false prophet. Mormonites, take your choice!

This prophet Smith, through his stone spectacles, wrote on the plates of Nephi, in his book of Mormon, every error and almost every truth discussed in N. York for the last ten years. He decides all the great controversies–infant baptism, ordination, the trinity, regeneration, repentance, justification, the fall of man, the atonement, transubstantiation, fasting, penance, church government, religious experience, the call to the ministry, the general resurrection, eternal punishment, who may baptize, and even the question of freemasonry, republican government, and the rights of man. All these topics are repeatedly alluded to. How much more benevolent and intelligent this American Apostle, than were the holy twelve, and Paul to assist them!!! He prophesied of all these topics, and of the apostasy, and infallibly decided, by his authority, every question. How easy to prophecy of the past or of the present time!!

But he is better skilled in the controversies in New York than in the geography or history of Judea. He makes John baptise in the village of Bethabara, and says Jesus was born in Jerusalem, p. 240. Great must be the faith of the Mormonites in this new Bible! The mariners compass was only known in Europe about 300 years ago; but Nephi knew all about steam boats and the compass 2400 years ago.

He represents the Christian institution as practiced among his Israelites before Jesus was born. And his Jews are called Christians while keeping the law of Moses, the holy Sabbath, and worshipping in their temple at their altars, and by their high priests.

28. From Whitmer's *An Address to All Believers in Christ*, 35.

29. Joseph Smith, *Book of Commandments* 44:31.

30. The Utah Mormons do not use Smith's revisions, claiming that it was not completed. Instead, they only use the King James Version for study.

31. Universalism teaches that all souls are saved and end up in heaven.

32. Found in *Doctrine and Covenants*, Section 89.

33. *Western Monitor* (Fayette, Missouri), August 2, 1833, quoted in Fawn M. Brodie, *No Man Knows My History* (New York: Random House, 1995), 133.

34. *Evening and Morning Star*, Vol. II, July 1833.

35. *Doctrine and Covenants*, Section 98.

36. It is possible that Joseph's interest in education was stimulated by the more academically inclined Sidney Rigdon, himself inspired by Alexander Campbell.

37. *Times and Seasons*, 5:614–617 (a Mormon journal published 1839–1846), available at www.centerplace.org/history/ts/.

38. For example, Fawn M. Brodie, in her book *No Man Knows My History*.

39. Wilhelm Wyl, *Mormon Portraits...Joseph Smith the Prophet, His Family and His Friends* (Salt Lake City: The Church of Jesus Christ of Latter-day Saints, 1886), 57.

40. From a previously unpublished letter in Fawn M. Brodie, *No Man Knows My History* (New York: Random House, 1995) 458–459.

41. *Doctrine and Covenants*, Section 111.

42. Joseph Smith, *The History of the Church*, 2:497.

43. *Doctrine and Covenants*, 116:1.

44. *The Life of Joseph Fielding Smith*, 340.

45. *History of the Church*, Vol. III, 180-181.

46. Though see also Judges 18.

47. As in Fawn M. Brodie, *No Man Knows My History*, 230. Brodie found this quote from Smith in George Hinkle and James B. Turner, *Correspondence, Orders, etc. in relation to the disturbances with the Mormons; and the evidence given before the Hon. Austin A. King, Judge of the Fifth Judicial Circuit of the State of Missouri, November 12, 1838* (Fayette, Missouri: General Assembly of Missouri, 1841).

48. William Swartzel, *Mormonism Exposed, being a journal of a residence in Missouri from 28th of May to 20th of August, 183* (Pekin Ohio, 1840), 29.

49. Joseph Smith, *History of the Church*, 5, 2.

50. Fawn M. Brodie, *No Man Knows My History* (New York: Vintage Books, 1995) 457–488.

51. There are many rumors of children fathered by Joseph Smith with his plural wives, including specific children who have been said to be from Joseph. Such charges are difficult to prove. Because Smith did not openly admit his polygamous relationships, we have no word from him claiming such children. We can conclude that Smith was probably but not certainly the father of children from his plural wives.

52. William Hepworth Dixon, *New America* (Philadelphia, 1867), 225.

53. Todd Compton, *Sacred Loneliness: The Plural Wives of Joseph Smith* (Salt Lake City: Signature Books, 1997).

54. *Doctrine and Covenants*, 132:4.

55. *Doctrine and Covenants*, 132:16–20.

56. *Doctrine and Covenants*, 132:20.

57. *Doctrine and Covenants*, 132:54.

58. As told by William Clayton, *Utah Historical Record*, Vol. VI, 224–226.

59. "Letter to the Saints," September 1, 1842, from *History of the Church*, Vol. V, 143.

60. Joseph Smith, *Millennial Star*, Vol. XXII, (1860), 455.

61. William Law, *Nauvoo Expositor*, June 7, 1844.

62. *History of the Church*, 7:233.

63. A list of evidence that Strang's letter was a forgery can be found in Stanley P. Hirshson, *The Lion of the Lord* (New York: Alfred A. Knopf. 1969), 56–57.

64. An estimate taken from the Saint Louis *American*, April 1, 1846.

65. *Doctrine and Covenants*, 84:18–28.

66. William Smith, *Warsaw Signal*, October 29, 1845.

67. Stanley P. Hirshson, *The Lion of the Lord* (Alfred A. Knopf, New York, 1969), 3.

68. Mary Van Sickle Wait: *Brigham Young in Cayuga County*, 1813-1819 (Ithaca: Dewitt Historical Society of Tompkins, County, New York, 1960), 5 This and many of the other references below are taken from Stanley P. Hirshson's book, *The Lion of the Lord*.

69. Orson F. Whitney, *Life of Heber C. Kimball* (Salt Lake City: Kimball Family), 35–36.

70. *Journal of Discourses*, IX, 219.

71. *Deseret News*, April 7, 1858; *Journal of Discourses*, VIII, 15–16.

72. *Journal of Discourses*, XII, 268.

73. Stanley P. Hirshson, *The Lion of the Lord* (New York: Alfred A. Knopf, 1969), 184–221.

74. New York *Herald*, January 10, 1852.

75. We have this account from Lee himself. The trustworthiness is debatable. However, the fact that he was later given three wives by Young and appointed probate judge supports the general veracity of Lee's account. *The Mountain Meadows Massacre, With the Life, Confession and Execution of John D. Lee, The Mormon* (Philadelphia: Barclay and Co., 1877), 1–28.

76. *Deseret News*, November 23, 1878.

77. New York *Tribune*, November 18, 1871.

78. *Journal of Discourses*, I 50.

79. New York *Tribune*, July 21, 1865. This quote is from a reporter who may be biased. However, many witnesses reported Young teaching this doctrine and other Presidents of the Latter-day Saints have confirmed the doctrine.

80. *New York Times*, May 25, 1857; New York *Tribune*, April 25, 1857.

81. See Stanley P. Hirshson, *The Lion of the Lord* (New York: Alfred A. Knopf, 1969), 124 for a list of scholarly studies.

82. Emphasis added. *Deseret News*, October 1, 1856.

83. *Deseret News*, February 8, 1857.

84. *History of the Church*, 4:461.

85. Joe Fields, unpublished. Adapted and used by permission.

86. Dr. Ross T. Christensen, *University Archaeological Society Newsletter*, no. 64, January 30, 1960, 5–6.

87. "Statement Regarding the Book of Mormon" Smithsonian Institution, Spring 1986.

88. Quoting from a letter from the National Geographic Society to the Tanners dated October 21, 1965, as cited in Jerald and Sandra Tanner, *Mormonism: Shadow or Reality?* (Salt Lake City: Modern Microfilm Company, 1982), 98.

89. *The Return*, Vol. II (August, 1890), 315.

90. Chloroform is the compound which was the primary one used to put people to sleep during surgery in the late 19th century. Quote taken from Mark Twain, *Roughing it—A Personal Narrative* (Berkeley: University of California Press, 1994).

91. Admittedly Luke 22:44 says nothing about blood issuing from Jesus' pores (a popular Christian tradition), only that his sweat fell *like* drops of blood to the ground. The point is that Smith has a prophecy of this Christian tradition in his book.

92. For more on the reliability of the New Testament text, see John Oakes, *Reasons for Belief* (Spring, Texas: IPI, 2005), ch. 6, and Douglas Jacoby, *Compelling Evidence for God and the Bible* (Eugene, Oregon: Harvest House, 2010), ch.5–7.

93. Orson Pratt, *Journal of Discourses*, 2:342.

94. Interestingly, the same passage in Deuteronomy is claimed by Muslim apologists as a prophecy of Muhammad!

95. Compiled by Joseph Fielding Smith, *Teachings of the Prophet Joseph Smith*, 370.

96. Joseph Smith, *History of the Church*, 6:303–5 *Teachings of the Prophet Joseph Smith*, 345-46).

97. Joseph Smith, *Journal of Discourses*, Vol. 1, 50.

98. Milton R. Hunter, *The Gospel Through the Ages*, (Salt Lake City: Steven and Walls, 1945), 15.

99. Joseph Smith, *History of the Church*, 5:254.

100. Brigham Young, *Journal of Discourses*, Vol. 9, 286.

101. Joseph Smith, *History of the Church*, Vol. 6, 302–317.

102. Compiled by Brigham Young, *Journal of Discourses*, Vol. 1, 345–46.

103. *Deseret News*, October 1, 1856, and February 8, 1857.

104. New York *Tribune*, July 21, 1865.

105. Journal of Discourses, 1:50.

106.

| Year | Estimated Membership (from official LDS records) |
|---|---|
| 1860 | 61,000 |
| 1870 | 90,000 |
| 1880 | 134,000 |
| 1890 | 188,000 |
| 1900 | 284,000 |
| 1910 | 398,000 |
| 1920 | 526,000 |
| 1930 | 670,000 |
| 1940 | 863,000 |
| 1950 | 1,110,000 |
| 1960 | 1,683,000 |
| 1970 | 2,931,000 |
| 1980 | 4,640,000 |
| 1990 | 7,961,000 |
| 2000 | 11,069,000 |
| 2010 | 14,131,000 |

107. Consider a few other statistics. In the April 2010 report to the General Council of the LDS Church there were 2865 stakes, 344 missions, 616 districts and 28,424 wards and branches. In Mormon vocabulary, a stake is an administrative unit, something like a Catholic diocese. A ward or branch is the equivalent of a single local church.

108. These numbers are unaudited and approximate. The Mormon Church stopped providing public information on their net worth in the 1960s.

109. Latayne Scott, *The Mormon Mirage* (Grand Rapids: Zondervan, 2009) , 207–215.

Latayne is a personal acquaintance. By a fortunate coincidence I taught Sunday School with her in Boulder, Colorado in 1981. She is perhaps the best-known former Mormon writer today.

110. This is accomplished by composing a genealogy for the believer which stretches back to a person of royal birth, who is assumed to be descended from a biblical figure.

111. The context for Paul's statements in 1 Corinthians 15 about baptisms for the dead is not certain. It is likely that he is speaking ironically about a false teaching the Corinthians had heard of. In any case, no scholars (except Mormon ones) agree that Paul is prescribing baptism for the dead in this passage.

112. Matthew 5:32, 19:9; Mark 10:11; Luke 16:18.

113. Jon Krakauer, *Under the Banner of Heaven* (New York: Anchor Books, 2005).

114. W. M. Paden, *Temple Mormonism—Its Evolution, Ritual and Meaning* (New York: A. J. Montgomery,1931), 18.

115. Jason Szep, "Fundamental Mormons Seek Recognition for Polygamy," Reuters, June 12, 2007.

116. David Ebershoff, *The Nineteenth Wife* (New York: Random House, 2008).

117. Jon Krakauer, *Under the Banner of Heaven: A Story of Violent Faith* (New York: Anchor Books, 2004).

118. D. Michael Quinn, quoted in Jerald and Sandra Tanner's *Distorted View of Mormonism: A Response to Mormonism—Shadow or Reality* (Salt Lake City: n.p., 1977).

119. James E. Talmadge, *The Articles of Faith* (Salt Lake City: The Church of Jesus Christ of Latter-day Saints, 1968), 7.

120. Latayne Scott, *The Mormon Mirage* (Grand Rapids, Michigan: Zondervan, 2009), 272.

121. Ibid., 264.

122. D. Michael Quinn, *The Mormon Hierarchy: Extensions of Power* (Salt Lake City: Signature Books, 1994), 129.

123. A book which can be used to prove that the Bible has not been changed is John Oakes, *Reasons for Belief: A Handbook of Christian Evidence* (Spring, Texas: IP Books, 2004).

124. For example, in 1981 the LDS authorized version of 2 Nephi 30:6 was changed. Formerly, it read, "...their scales of darkness shall begin to fall from their eyes; and many generations shall not pass away among them, save they shall be a white and delightsome people." The revised edition replaced the offensive "white and delightsome" to the less offensive "pure and delightsome." Remember that this is not a change in translation. It is a change in a supposedly inspired version of the Bible—"the most perfect of any book."

125. Unpublished. Used by permission.

# Appendix: Delusions

An analysis of the Book of Mormon with an examination of its internal and external evidences, and a refutation of its pretenses to divine authority.

by Alexander Campbell, February 10, 1831

*Editor's Note: What makes this expose powerful is that it was written within a year of the release of the Book of Mormon. Some introductory material has been removed for brevity sake.* —Dr. John M. Oakes

Since the Millennium and the evils of sectarianism have been the subjects of much speaking and writing, impostures have been numerous. In the memory of the present generation, many delusions have been propagated and received. The shakers, a sect instituted by Anna Lesse, in 1774, have not yet quite dwindled away. This elect Lady, as they style her, was the head of this party, and gave them a new bible. "They assert that she spoke seventy-two languages, and conversed with the dead. Through her all blessings flow to her followers—she appointed the sacred dance and the fantastic song, and consecrated shivering, swooning and falling down, acts of acceptable devotion. They are for a common stock, and rank marriage among the works of the flesh,—they are plain in their apparel, and assume the aspect of the friars and nuns of Catholic superstition."

The Barkers, Jumpers, and Mutterers of the present age, need not be mentioned here. Nor need we detail the history of Miss Campbell, who in Good Old Scotland a year or two since came back from the dead and had the gift of tongues, who was believed in by several ministers of the Scotch Church. But we shall proceed to notice the most recent and the most impudent delusion which has appeared in our time. The people that have received this imposture are called, THE MORMONITES. I have just examined their bible, and will first notice its contents. It is called the "Book of Mormon", an account written by the hand of Mormon upon plates taken from the plains of Nephi, wherefore it is an abridgement of the record of the people of Nephi, and also of the Lamanites, written to the Lamanites, which are a remnant of the House of Israel, and also to Jew and Gentile. Written by way of commandment, and also by the spirit of prophecy and of Revelation—By Joseph Smith, Junior, Author and proprietor. From plates dug out of the earth, in the township of Manchester, Ontario, New York.—Palmyra, printed by E.B. Grandin, for the Author, 1830. It is a collection of books said to have been written by different persons during the interval of 1020 years—the 1st and second books of Nephi occupy 122 pages; the Book of Jacob, the brother of Nephi occupies 21; that of Enos 3; that of Jarom 2; that of Omin 4; the words of Mormon 3; the book of Mosiah 68; that of Alma 186; that of Helaman 44; that of Nephi the son of Helaman 66; that of Mormon 20; that of Ether 35; and that of Morom 14 pages; making in all 588 octavo pages.

This romance—but this is for it a name too innocent—begins with the religious adventures of one Lehi, whose wife was Sariah, and their four sons, Laman, Lemuel, Sam, and Nephi. Lehi lived in Jerusalem all his life, up to the first year of Zedekiah, King of Judah, and when the prophets appeared foretelling the utter destruction of Jerusalem, Lehi humbled himself, and after various visions and revelations, started with his sons into the wilderness. Lehi, before his departure, forgot to bring with him the records of his family, and that of the Jews; but Nephi, his younger son, with much pious courage returned and succeeded in getting upon plates of brass the records of the Jews from the creation down to the first year of Zedekiah, King of Judah, and also the prophets including many prophecies delivered by Jeremiah.

From the records it appeared that this Lehi was a son of Joseph. He prevailed on one Ishmael and his family to accompany him into the wilderness, whose daughters the sons of Lehi took for wives.

Lehi was a greater prophet than any of the Jewish prophets, and uttered all the events of the Christian era, and developed the records of Matthew, Luke, and John, six hundred years before John the Baptist was born.—These pilgrims travelled several days journey in some wilderness, "a south, south-east direction, along the borders of the Red Sea." A ball with pointers on it, inscribed with various intelligence, legible at proper times, was the pillar and index in passing through the wilderness for many, very many days. By their bow and arrow they lived for eight years, travelling an easterly course from Jerusalem, until they came to a great sea. By divine revelation Nephi constructed a ship, and although opposed by his unbelieving brethren, being greatly assisted by the Holy Spirit, he succeeded in launching her safely, and got all his tribe, with all their stock of seeds, animals, and provisions, safely aboard. They had "a compass" which none but Nephi knew how to manage; but the Lord had promised them a fine land, and after many perils and trials, and a long passage, they safely arrived in the land of promise. Nephi made brazen plates soon after his arrival in America, for that was the land of promise to them, and on these plates be marked their peregrinations and adventures, and all the prophecies which God gave to him concerning the future destinies of his people, and the human race.

After his father's death, his brethren rebelled against him. They finally separated in the wilderness, and became the heads of different tribes, often in the lapse of generations making incurations upon each other. The Nephites, like their father, for many generations were good Christians, believers in the doctrines of the Calvinists and Methodists, and preaching baptism and other Christian usages hundreds of years before Jesus Christ was born!

Before Nephi died, which was about fifty-five years from the flight of Lehi from Jerusalem, he had preached to his people everything which is now preached in the state of New York, and anointed or ordained his brother Enos "in the nurture and admonition of the Lord," gave him the plates, and left him successor in office over the people of Nephi. Enos says "there came a voice to me, saying, Enos thy sins are forgiven thee, and thou shalt be blessed. And, I sayeth, Lord how it is done. And he sayeth unto me, Because of thy faith in Christ, whom thou hast not heard nor seen" (p. 143). Enos died one hundred seventy-nine years from the hegira of Lehi; consequently, this happened four hundred thirty-one years before Jesus Christ was born. He was a contemporary with Nehemiah, and may we not say how much wiser and more enlightened were the Nephites in America than the Jews at their return to Jerusalem! Enos gave the plates to Jarom, his son. In his time "they kept the law of Moses and the Sabbath day holy to the Lord." During the priesthood and reign of Enos, there were many commotions and wars between his people and the Lamanites. Then the sharp pointed arrow, the quiver, and the dart were invented. Jarom delivered his plates to his son Omni, and gave up the ghost two hundred thirty-eight years from the flight of Lehi. Omni died two hundred seventy-six from the hegira, and gave the plates to his son Amaron, who in the year three hundred and twenty, gave them to his brother Chemish; he, to his son Abinadom; he to his son Amaleki; and he having no son, gave them to the just and pious King Benjamin. King Benjamin had three sons, Mosiah, Helorum, and Helaman, whom he educated in all the learning of his fathers. To Mosiah he delivered up the plates of Nephi, the ball which guided them through the wilderness, and the sword of one Laban, of mighty renown. King Benjamin addressed his people from the new temple which they had erected, for they had, even then, built a temple, synagogues, and a tower, in the New World.

King Benjamin assembled the people to sacrifice according to the law around the new temple; and he enjoined upon them, at the same time, the Christian institutions, and gave them a Patriarchal valedictory. After they had heard him speak, and had offered up their sacrifices, they fell down and prayed in the following words: "'O have mercy, and apply the atoning blood of Christ, that we may receive forgiveness of our sins, and our hearts may be purified; for we believe in Jesus Christ the son of God, who created heaven and earth and all things, who shall come down upon the children of men.' Then the spirit of the Lord fell upon them and they were filled with joy, having received a remission of their sins" (p. 162).

King Benjamin ordered his people to take upon them the name of Christ, and in these remarkable words, "There is no other name given whereby salvation cometh; therefore I would that you should take upon you the name of Christ, all you that have entered into the covenant with God that ye should be obedient unto the end of your lives" (p. 166). They all took upon them the name of Christ, and he having ordained them priests and teachers, and appointed his son, Mosiah, to reign in his stead, gave up the Ghost 476 years after Lehi's escape from Jerusalem, and one hundred twenty-four before Christ was born, Mosiah gave up the plates of brass, and all the things which we had kept, to Alma the son of Alma, who was appointed "chief judge and high priest," the people willing to have no king, and Mosiah died five hundred sixty-nine years from the time Lehi left Jerusalem.

In the 14th year of the Judges, and 69 years before the birth of Jesus, they sent out missionary priests, who preached through all the tribes of the country against all vices, holding "forth the coming of the soul of

God, his sufferings, death and resurrection, and that he should appear unto them after his resurrection: and this the people did hear with great joy and gladness." (p. 268).

Alma's book reaches down to the end of the 39th year of the Judges. These were wonderful years- many cities were founded, many battles were fought, fortifications reared, letters written, and even in one year a certain Hagoth built an exceeding large ship, and launched it forth into the west sea. in this embarked many of the Nephites. This same ship-builder the next year built other ships, one was lost with all its passengers and crew (p.406).

Many prophecies were pronounced; one that in 400 years after the coming of Christ, the Nephites would lose their religion. During the time of the Judges, many were called Christians by name, and "baptism unto repentance" was a common thing. "And it came to pass that they did appoint priests and teachers through all the land, and over all the churches." (p. 349). "And those who did belong to the church were faithful, yea all those who were true believers in Christ took upon them gladly the name of Christ, or Christians, as they were called, because of their belief in Christ" (p. 301). "And it came to pass that there were many who died firmly believing that their souls were redeemed by the Lord Jesus Christ: thus they went out of the world rejoicing" (p. 353). The word was preached by Helaman, Shiblon, Corianton, Amnon, and his brethren, yea and all those, who had been ordained by the holy order of God, being baptized unto repentance, and sent forth to preach unto the people" (p. 623). This happened in the nineteenth year of the Judges, seventy-two years before the birth of Jesus. Before this time synagogues with pulpits were built, "for the Zoramites," a sort of Episcopalians, "gathered themselves together on one day of the week, which day they called the day of the Lord." "And they had a place which was high and lifted up, which held but one man, who read prayers, the same prayers every week; and this high place was called Rameumpton, which being interpreted, is the holy stand" (p. 311). The book of Helaman reacheth down to the ninetieth year of the Judges, and to the year preceding that in which the Messiah was born. During the period embraced in Helaman's narrative, many ten thousands were baptized. "And behold the holy spirit of God did come down from heaven, and did enter into their hearts, and they were filled as with fire, and they could speak forth marvelous words" (p. 421).

Masonry was invented about this time; for men began to bind themselves in secret oaths to aid one another in all things, good or evil (p. 424). Powers of loosing and binding in heaven were conferred upon Nephi, the son of Helaman, and all miraculous power, such as the apostles possessed. One Samuel, also foretold that "the Christ would be born in five years, and that the night before should be as light as day; and that the day of his death should be a day of darkness like the night" (p. 445). The book of this Nephi commences with the birth of the Messiah, six hundred years from the departure of Lehi from Jerusalem. In the midst of the threats of the infidels to slaughter the faithful, the sun set; but lo! the night was clear as mid-day, and from that period they changed their era, and counted time as we do. A star also appeared, but it is not stated how it could be seen in a night as bright as day; but it was universally seen throughout all the land, to the salvation of the pious from the threats of their enemies. The terrors of the day of his death are also stated, and in the thirty-fourth year from his nativity, after his resurrection, he descended from heaven and visited the people of Nephi. Jesus called upon them to examine his hands and his sides, as he did Thomas, though none of them had expressed a doubt. Two thousand five hundred men, women and children, one by one, examined him, and then worshipped him. He commanded Nephi to baptize, and gave him the words which he was to use, viz: "Having authority given me, of Jesus Christ, I baptize you in the name of the Father and of the Son, and of the Holy Ghost. Amen." He commissioned eleven others, who with Nephi, were his twelve American Apostles, and promised himself to baptize their converts "with fire and with the Holy Spirit."

He delivers them the sermon upon the mount, and some other sayings recorded in Matthew, Mark, Luke, and John; He healed all their diseases, and prayed for their children; but the things spoken were so great and marvelous that they could not be spoken nor written.

He ordained one to administer the supper, who alone had authority to dispense it to the disciples baptized in his name. The only new commandments which were given to the American Christians on his occasional visits which were repeated, were—"Pray in your families unto the Father, always in my name, that your wives and your children may be blessed." "Meet often, and forbid no man from coming unto you when you shall meet together" (p. 492).

Nephi was chief among the twelve apostles: he baptized himself, and then baptized the eleven, whose names were Timothy, Jonas, Mathoni and Mathoninah, Kumen, Kumenonhi, Jeremiah, Shimnon, Jonas, Zedekiah, and Isaiah, "They were baptized in fire and the Holy Ghost." Not a new word, however, should be written in addition to those found in the New Testament; for although he spake for several days to these American disciples, none of the new and marvelous sayings could be uttered or written! He inspected the plates of Nephi, and only found one omission, which was that he failed to mention the resurrection of many saints in America at the time of the tempest and earthquake. He commanded these Nephites to be called Christians. The book of Nephi the son of Nephi, gives, in four pages, the history of 320 years after Christ. In the thirty-sixth year, all the inhabitants of the land were converted; there was a perfect community and no disputations in the land for one hundred seventy years. Three of the American apostles were never to die, and were seen four hundred years after Christ; but what has become of them no one can tell, except Cowdery, Whitmer and Harris, the three witnesses of the truth of the plates of Nephi, be these three immortal men. Towards the close of the history of Nephi or the record Ammaron, sects and divisions and battles became frequent, and all goodness had almost left the continent in the year three hundred and twenty.

Mormon appears next in the drama, the recording angel of the whole matter, who, by the way, was a mighty general and great Christian; he commanded in one engagement forty-two thousand men against the Lamanites! He was no Quaker! This dreadful battle was fought A.D. 330. The Lamanites took South America for themselves, and gave North America to the Nephites. Mormon was very orthodox, for he preached in these words, A.D. 362: "That Jesus was the very Christ and the very God." He must have heard of the Arian controversy by some angel!!

Moroni finishes what Mormon his father, left undone, and continues the history, till A.D. 400. He pleads that no one shall disbelieve his record because of its imperfections!! and declares that none who receive it will condemn it on account of its imperfections, and for not doing so, the same shall know greater things (p. 532). "He that condemneth it shall be in danger of hell fire." He laments the prevalence of free masonry in the times when his book should be dug up out of the earth, and proves that miracles will never cease; because God is the same yesterday, to day, and forever—consequently must always create suns, moons, and stars, every day!! He exhorted to "take heed that none be baptized without telling their experience, nor partake of the sacrament of Christ unworthily?!! (p. 537). Moroni, in the conclusion of his book of Mormon, says if his plates had been larger we should have written in Hebrew; but because of this difficulty he wrote in the "Reformed Egyptian," being handed down and altered unto us according to our manner of speech (p. 538). "Condemn me not," says he, "because of mine imperfections; neither my father, because of his imperfections, neither them which have written before him; but rather give thanks unto God that he hath made manifest unto you our imperfections, that you may learn to be more wise than we have been" (p. 538). A very necessary advice, indeed!!

Moroni writes the book of Ether, containing an account of the people of Jared, who escaped from the building of the tower of Babel unconfounded in his language. "These people of Jared, God marched before in a cloud, and directed them through the wilderness, and instructed them to build barges to cross seas; and finally they built eight barges, air tight, and were commanded to make a hole in the top to admit air, and one in the bottom to admit water, and in them were put sixteen windows of molten stone, which when touched by the finger of Jesus, became as transparent as glass, and gave them light under 'the mountain waves,' and when above the water. He that touched these stones, appeared unto the brother of Jared, and said, behold I am Jesus Christ, I am the father and the son." Two of these stones were sealed up with the plates and became the spectacles of Joseph Smith, according to a prediction uttered before Abraham was born. It was also foretold in the book of Ether, written by Moroni, that he that should find the plates should have the privilege of showing the plates unto those who shall assist to bring forth this work, and unto three shall they be shown by the power of God: wherefore they shall of a surety known that these things are true (p. 548).

And the eight barges, air-tight, made like ducks, after swimming and diving 334 days, arrived on the coasts of the land of promise. The book of Ether relates the wars and carnage amongst these people. In the lapse of generations, they counted two millions of mighty men, besides women and children, slain; and finally, they were all killed but one, and he fell to the earth as if he had no life. So ends the book of Ether (p. 573).

The book of Moroni details the manner of ordaining priests and teachers, the manner of administering ordinances, and the epistles of Mormon to his soon Moroni. Moroni seal up the record A.D. 420, and assures the world that spiritual gifts shall never cease, only through unbelief. And when the plates of Nephi should be dug out of the earth, he declares that men should ask God the Eternal Father, in the name of Christ, "If these things were not true." "If with a sincere heart and real intent, having faith in Christ, such prayers are made, ye shall know the truth of all things" (p. 586). The testimony of Oliver Cowdery, David Whitmer, and Martin Harris, asserting that they saw the plates, is appended. They also testify that they know that they have been translated by the gift and power of God, for his voice has declared it unto them. Another testimony is appended signed by four Whitmers, one Hiram Page, and three Smiths, affirming that they saw the plates, handled them, and that Smith has got the plates in his possession.

Such is an analysis of the book of Mormon, the bible of the Mormonites. For noticing of which I would have asked forgiveness from all my readers, had not several hundred persons of different denominations believed in it. On this account alone has it become necessary to notice it, and for the same reason we must examine its pretensions to divine authority; for it purports to be a revelation from God. And in the first place, we shall examine its internal evidences.

## Internal Evidences

It admits the Old and New Testaments to contain the revelations, institutions and commandments of God to Patriarchs, Jews, and Gentiles, down to the year 1830, and always, as such, speaks of them and quotes them. This admission at once blasts its pretensions to credibility. Admitting the bible now received to have come from God, it is impossible that the book of Mormon came from the same author. For the following reasons:

**1. Smith, its real author, as ignorant and impudent a knave as ever wrote a book, betrays the cloven foot in basing his whole book upon a false fact, or a pretended fact, which makes God a liar.** It is this: With the Jews, God made a covenant at Mount Sinai, and instituted a priesthood and a high priesthood. The priesthood he gave to the tribe of Levi, and the high priesthood to Aaron and his sons for an everlasting priesthood. He separated Levi, and covenanted to give him this office irrevocably while ever the temple stood, or till the Messiah came. "Then, says God Moses shall appoint Aaron and his sons, and they shall wait on their priest's office, and the stranger, (the person of another family,) who cometh nigh, shall be put to death" (Numbers 3:10). "And the priests, the sons of Levi, shall come near; for them the Lord thy God hath chosen to minister unto him, and to bless in the name of the Lord, and by their word shall every controversy and every stroke be tried" (Deut. 21:5). Korah, Dathan, and Abiram, with 250 men of renown, rebelled against a part of the institution of the priesthood, and the Lord destroyed them in the presence of the whole congregation. This was to be a memorial that no stranger invade any part of the office of the priesthood (Numbers 16:40). Fourteen thousand and seven hundred of the people were destroyed by a plague for murmuring against this memorial.

In the 18th chapter of Numbers the Levites are again given to Aaron and his sons, and the priesthood confirmed to them with this threat "The stranger that cometh night shall be put to death." Even Jesus, says Paul, were he on earth, could not be a priest, for he was of a tribe concerning which Moses spake nothing of priesthood (Hebrews 7:13). So irrevocable was the grant of the priesthood to Levi, and of the high priesthood to Aaron, that no stranger dare approach the altar of God which Moses established. Hence, Jesus himself was excluded from officiating as priest on earth according to the law.

This Joseph Smith overlooked in his impious fraud, and makes his hero Lehi spring from Joseph. And just as soon as his sons return with the roll of his lineage, ascertaining that he was of the tribe of Joseph, he and his sons acceptably "offer sacrifices and burnt offerings to the Lord" (p. 15). Also it is repeated, (p. 18). Nephi became chief artificer, ship-builder and mariner; was scribe, prophet, priest and king unto his own people, and "consecrated Jacob and Joseph", the sons of his father, priests to God and teachers–almost six hundred years before the fullness of the times of the Jewish economy was completed (p. 72). Nephi represents himself withal as "under the law of Moses," (p. 105). They build a temple in the new world, and in 55 years after they leave Jerusalem, make a new priesthood which God approbates. A high priest is also consecrated, and yet they are all the while "teaching the law of Moses, and exhorting the people to keep it!" (p. 146, 209).

Thus God is represented as instituting, approbating and blessing a new priesthood from the tribe of Joseph, concerning which Moses gave no commandment concerning priesthood. Although God had promised in the law of Moses, that if any man, not of the tribe and family of Levi and Aaron, should approach the office of priest, he would surely die; he is represented by Smith as blessing, approbating, and sustaining another family in this approbated office. The God of Abraham or Joseph Smith must then be a liar!! And who will hesitate to pronounce him an imposter? This lie runs through his records for the first six hundred years of his story.

**2. This ignorant and impudent liar, in the next place, makes the God of Abraham, Isaac and Jacob, violate his covenants with Israel and Judah, concerning the land of Canaan, by promising a new land to the pious Jew.**

If a company of reprobate Jews had departed from Jerusalem and the temple, in the days of Zedekiah, and founded a new colony, it would not have been so incongruous. But to represent God as inspiring a devout Jew and a prophet, such as Levi and Nephi are represented by Smith, with a resolution to forsake Jerusalem and God's own house, and to depart from the land which God swore to their fathers so long as they were obedient; and to guide by a miracle and to bless by prodigies a good man in forsaking God's covenant and worship—is so monstrous an error, that language fails to afford a name for it. It is to make God violate his own covenants, and set at naught his own promises, and to convert his own curses into blessings. Excision from the commonwealth of Israel, and banishment from Jerusalem and the temple, were the greatest curses the law of Moses knew. But Smith makes a good and pious Jew the subject of this curse, and sends him off into the inhospitable wilderness, disinherits him in Canaan, and makes him more happy in forsaking the institutions of Moses, more intelligent in the wilderness, and more prosperous in adversity, than even the Jews in their best days, in the best of lands, and under the best of all governments!!! The imposter was too ignorant of the history of the Jews and the nature of the covenants of promise, to have even alluded to them in his book, if he had not supposed that he had the plates of Moses in his own keeping, as he had his "molten plates" of Nephi. To separate a family from the nation of Israel, was to accumulate all the curses of the law upon that family (Deut. 29:21).

**3. He has more of the Jews, living in the new world, than could have been numbered anywhere else, even in the days of John the Baptist; and has placed them under a new dynasty**. The scepter, with him, has departed from Judah, and a lawgiver from among his descendants, hundreds of years before Shiloh came; and king Benjamin is a wiser and more renowned king than King Solomon. He seems to have gone upon an adage which saith, "the more marvelous, the more credible the tale," and the less of fact, and the more of fiction, the more intelligible and reasonable the narrative.

**4. He represents the temple worship as continued in his new land of promise contrary to every precept of the law, and so happy are the people of Nephi as never to shed a tear on account of the excision, nor turn an eye toward Jerusalem or God's temple.** The pious Jews in their captivity turned their faces to Jerusalem and the holy place, and remembered God's promises concerning the place where he recorded his name. They hung their harps upon the willow, and could not sing the songs of Zion in a foreign land; but the Nephites have not a single wish for Jerusalem, for they can, in their wigwam temple, in the wilderness of America, enjoy more of God's presence than the most righteous Jew could enjoy in that house of which David had rather be a doorkeeper, than to dwell in the tabernacles of men. And all this too, when God's only house of prayer, according to his covenant with Israel, stood in Jerusalem.

**5. Malachi, the last of the Jewish prophets, commanded Israel to regard the law of Moses till the Messiah came.** And Moses commanded them to regard him till the Great Prophet came. But Nephi and Smith's prophets institute ordinances and observances for the Jews, subversive of Moses, 500 years before the Great Prophet came.

**6. Passing over a hundred similar errors, we shall next notice his ignorance of the New Testament matters and things.** The twelve Apostles of the Lamb, are said by Paul, to have developed certain secrets, which were hid for ages and generations, which Paul says were ordained before the world to their glory, that they should have the honor of announcing them. But Smith makes his pious hero Nephi, 600 years before the Messiah began to preach, and disclose these secrets concerning the calling of the Gentiles, and the blessings flowing through the Messiah to Jews and Gentiles, which Paul says were hid for ages and generations, "which in these ages was not made known unto the sons of men, as it is now revealed unto us the holy Apostles and prophets, by the spirit; that the Gentiles should be fellow heirs and of the same body and partakers of his promise in Christ by the Gospel." Smith makes Nephi express every truth found in the writings of the Apostles concerning the calling and blessing of the Gentiles, and even quotes the 11th chapter of Romans, and many other passages before he had a son grown in the wilderness able to aim an arrow at a deer. Paul says these things were secrets and unknown until his time; but Smith makes Nephi say the same things 600 years before Paul was converted! One of the two is a false prophet. Mormonites, take your choice!

**7. This prophet Smith, through his stone spectacles, wrote on the plates of Nephi, in his book of Mormon, every error and almost every truth discussed in New York for the last ten years.** He decides all the great controversies—infant baptism, ordination, the trinity, regeneration, repentance, justification, the fall of man, the atonement, transubstantiation, fasting, penance, church government, religious experience, the call to the ministry, the general resurrection, eternal punishment, who may baptize, and even the question of freemasonry, republican government, and the rights of man. All these topics are repeatedly alluded to. How much more benevolent and intelligent this American Apostle, than were the holy twelve, and Paul to assist them!!! He prophesied of all these topics, and of the apostasy, and infallibly decided, by his authority, every question. How easy to prophecy of the past or of the present time!!

**8. But he is better skilled in the controversies in New York than in the geography or history of Judea.** He makes John baptize in the village of Bethabara, (p. 22) and says Jesus was born in Jerusalem (p. 240). Great must be the faith of the Mormonites in this new Bible!!! The mariners compass was only known in Europe about 300 years ago; but Nephi knew all about steam boats and the compass 2400 years ago.

**9. He represents the Christian institution as practiced among his Israelites before Jesus was born.** And his Jews are called Christians while keeping the law of Moses, the holy Sabbath, and worshipping in their temple at their altars, and by their high priests.

**10. But not to honor him by a too minute examination and exposition, I will sum up the whole of the internal evidence which I deem worthy of remark, in the following details:**

The book professes to be written at intervals and by different persons during the long period of 1020 years. And yet for uniformity of style, there never was a book more evidently written by one set of fingers, nor more certainly conceived in one cranium since the first book appeared in human language, than this same book. If I could swear to any man's voice, face or person, assuming different names, I could swear that this book was written by one man. And as Joseph Smith is a very ignorant man and is called the author on the title page, I cannot doubt for a single moment that he is the sole author and proprietor of it. As a specimen of his style the reader will take the following samples.

Page 4. In his own preface: "The plates of which hath been spoken." In the last page, "the plates of which hath been spoken." In the certificate signed by Cowdery and his two witnesses, he has the same idiom, "which came from the tower of which hath been spoken;" Page 16, "we are a descendant of Joseph." "The virgin which thou seest is the mother of God." "Behold the Lamb of God the Eternal Father," p. 25; "Ye are like unto they," "and I saith unto them," (p. 44). "We did arrive to the promised land;" (p. 49), "made mention upon the first plate" (p. 50).

Nephi 2400 years ago hears the saying of a Pagan who lived 634 years after him, "The God of nature suffers" (p. 51). "The righteous need not fear, for it is they which shall not be confounded" (p. 58). Shakespeare was read by Nephi 2200 years before he was born, "The silent grave from whence no traveller returns" (p. 61). "Your own eternal welfare" was a phrase then common in America (p. 62). "Salvation is free" was then announced. "That Jesus should rise from the dead" was repeatedly declared on this continent in the reign of Nebuchadnezzar. And at the same time it was said, "Messiah cometh in the fullness of time that he might redeem the children of men from the fall" (p. 65). "The fall" was frequently spoken of at the Isthmus of Darien 2400 years ago.

I had no object, says Nephi, in the reign of Zedekiah, "but the everlasting salvation of your souls" (p. 66). "I had spake many things," 'for a more history part are written upon mine other plates'" (p. 69). "Do not anger again because of mine enemies" (p. 70). "For it behoveth the Great Creator that he die for all men." "It must needs be an infinite atonement." "This flesh must go to its mother earth." "And this death must deliver up its dead" (p. 70), were common phrases 2300 years ago—"for the atonement satisfieth the demands of his justice upon all those who have not the law given them" (p. 81). The Calvinists were in America before Nephi.

"The Lord remembereth all they" (p. 85). "The atonement is infinite for all mankind" (p .104). The Americans knew this on the Columbo 2400 years ago. "His name shall be called Jesus Christ the Son of God." An angel told this to Nephi 545 years before it was told to Mary (p. 105). "And they shall teach with their learning and deny the Holy Ghost which giveth them utterance;" this prophecy was at that time delivered against us (p. 112). "My words shall hiss forth unto the ends of the earth" (p. 115). "Wherein did the Lamb of God fill all the righteousness in being baptized by water" (p. 118). This question was discussed 2300 years ago. "The baptism by fire and the Holy Ghost was preached in the days of Cyrus" (p. 119). "The only true doctrine of the Father and of the Son and of the Holy Ghost which is one God without end. Amen" (p. 120). This was decided in the time of Daniel the Prophet. "I glory in plainness," says Nephi. "Christ will show you that these are his words in the last day" (p. 122). Too late to prove your mission, Mr. Nephi!

"After that ye have obtained a hope in Christ, ye shall obtain riches if you seek them." So spoke Jacob in the days of Ezekiel the Prophet. "They believed in Christ and worshipped the Father in his name" (p. 129). This was said by Jacob in the time of Daniel. "Do as ye hath hitherto done," says Mosiah (p. 158). These Smith-isms are in every page. "And his mother shall be called Mary" (p. 160). "The Son of God and Father of heaven and earth" (p. 161). "The infant perisheth not, that dieth in his infancy." "For the natural man is an enemy of God and was from the fall of Adam, and will be forever and ever" (p. 161). This was spoken by King Benjamin 124 years before Christ. He was a Yankee, too, for he spoke like Smith, saying, "I who ye call your king." "They saith unto the king" (p. 182). This was another Joseph Smith called Mosiah. "They were baptized in the waters of Mormon, and were called the church of Christ" (p. 192). This happened 100 years before Christ was born. "Alma, why persecuteth thou the church of God" (p. 222). "Ye must be born again; yea, born of God—changed from their carnal and fallen state to a state of righteousness" (p. 214). This was preached also 100 years before Christ was born. "These things had not ought to be" (p. 220).

"I, Alma, being consecrated by my father Alma to be a high priest over the church of God, he having power and authority from God to do these things (p. 232) say unto you, except ye repent ye can in no wise enter into the Kingdom of Heaven" (p. 237). "He ordained priests and elders, by laying on his hands, to watch over the church"—"Not so much as a hair of the head shall be lost in the grave"—"The holy order of the high priesthood" (p. 250). The high priesthood of Alma was about 80 years before Christ. "The Lord poured out his spirit to prepare the minds of the people for the preaching of Alma, preaching repentance" (p. 268). Alma was a Yankee of Smith's school, for he saith: "The light of everlasting light was lit up in his soul" (p. 47).

During the pontificate of Alma men prayed thus: "If there is a God, and if thou art God wilt thou make thyself known unto me" (p. 286). Alma "clapped his hands upon all they which were with him" (p. 313). "Instruments in the hand of God" were the preachers of Alma (p. 323). Modest and orthodox men, truly! "If ye deny the Holy Ghost when it once hath place in you, and ye know that ye deny, behold this is the unpardonable sin" (p. 332). So Alma preached. "And now my son, ye are called of God to preach the Gospel" (p. 340). "They were high priests over the church" (p. 350). "The twenty and second year of the Judges this came to pass" (p. 364). "They were valiant for courage" (p. 376).

These are but as one drop out of a bucket compared with the amount of Smith-isms in this book. It is patched up and cemented with "And it came to pass"—"I sayeth unto you"—"Ye saith unto him"—and all the King James' HATHS, DIDS and DOTHS—in the lowest imitation of the common version; and is, without exaggeration, the meanest book in the English language; but it is a translation made through stone spectacles, in a dark room, and in the hat of the prophet Smith from the REFORMED EGYPTIAN!! It has not one good sentence in it, save the profanation of those sentences quoted from the Oracles of the living God. I would as soon compare a bat to the American eagle, a mouse to a mammoth, or the deformities of a specter to the beauties of Him whom John saw in Patmos, as to contrast it with a single chapter in all the writings of the Jewish or Christian prophets. It is as certainly Smith's fabrication as Satan is the father of lies, or darkness the offspring of night. So much for the internal evidences of the Book of Mormon.

## External Evidences

Its external evidences are, first, the testimony of the prophets Cowdery, Whitmer, and Harris; who saw the plates and heard the voice of God; who are disinterested retailers of the books. I would ask them how they knew that it was God's voice which they heard—but they would tell me to ask God in faith. THAT IS, I MUST BELIEVE IT FIRST, AND THEN ASK GOD IF IT BE TRUE! 'Tis better to take Nephi's proof which is promised to us in the day of final judgment! They say that spiritual gifts are continued to the end of time among the true believers. They are true believers—have they wrought any miracles? They have tried, but their faith failed. Can they show any spiritual gift? Yes, they can mutter Indian and traffic in new Bibles.

"But Smith is the wonder of the world." So was the Apocalyptic beast! "An ignorant young man." That needs no proof. Gulliver's Travels is a heroic problem in comparison of this book of Smith. "But he cannot write a page." Neither could Mahomet, who gave forth the Koran. "Smith is an honest looking fellow." So was Simon Magus, the sorcerer. "But he was inspired." So was Judas, by Satan.

Its external evidences are also the subscriptions of four Whitmers, three Smiths, and one Page, the relatives and connections of Joseph Smith, junior. And these "men handled as many of the brazen or golden leaves as the said Smith translated." So did I. But Smith has got the plates of which hath been spoken. Let him show them. Their certificate proves nothing, save that Smith wrote it, and they signed it. But Smith gives testimony himself. There is one who says, "If I bear testimony of myself, my testimony ought not to be regarded."

If this prophet and his three prophetic witnesses had aught of speciosity about them or their book, we would have examined it and exposed it in a different manner. I have never felt myself so fully authorized to address mortal man in the style in which Paul addressed Elymas the sorcerer as I feel towards this Atheist Smith. His three witnesses, I am credibly informed, on one of their horse-swapping and prophetic excursions in the Sandusky country, having bartered horses three times for once preaching, represented Walter Scott and myself as employed in translating these plates, and as believers in the book of Mormon. If there was anything plausible about Smith, I would say to those who believe him to be a prophet, hear the question which Moses put into the mouth of the Jews, and his answer to it—"And if thou say in thine heart, HOW SHALL WE KNOW THE WORD WHICH THE LORD HATH NOT SPOKEN?"—Does he answer, "ASK THE LORD AND HE WILL TELL YOU?"—Does he say "Wait till the day of judgment and you will know?" Nay, indeed; but—"When a prophet speaketh in the name of the Lord, if the thing follow not nor come to pass, that is the thing which the Lord hath not spoken; the prophet hath spoken it presumptuously: THOU SHALT NOT BE AFRAID OF HIM" (Deut. 18:8). Smith has failed in every instance to verify one of his own sayings. Again, I would say in the words of the Lord by Isaiah, "Bring forth your strong reasons, saith the King of Jacob: let them bring them forth and show us what shall happen: let them show the former things what they mean, that we may consider them, and know the latter end of them—show the things which are to come hereafter, that we may know that you are prophets: yea, do good or do evil, that we may be dismayed and behold it together. Behold you are nothing, and your work of naught: an abomination is every one that chooseth you" (Isaiah 41:21-23).

Let the children of Mormon ponder well, if yet reason remains with them, the following passage from Isaiah 44; and if they cannot see the analogy between themselves and the sons of ancient imposture, then reason is of as little use to them as it was to those of whom the prophet spake:

"The carpenters having chosen a piece of wood framed it by rule and glued the parts together, and made it in the form of a man, and with the comeliness of a man, to set it in a house. He cut wood from the forest which the Lord planted—a pine tree, which the rain had nourished, that it might be fuel for the use of man: and having taken some of it he warmed himself; and with other pieces they made a fire and baked cakes, and of the residue they made gods and worshipped them. Did he not burn half of it in the fire, and, with the coals of that half bake cakes: and having roasted meat with it did he not eat and was satisfied; and when warmed say, "Aha! I am warmed, I have enjoyed the fire?" Yet of the residue he made a carved god, and worshipped it, and prayeth to it, saying, "Deliver me, for thou art my God."

'They had not sense to think; for they were so involved in darkness that they could not see with their eyes, nor understand with their hearts: nor did any reason in his mind, nor by his understanding recollect, that he had burned half of it in the fire, and on the coals thereof baked cakes, and had roasted flesh and eaten, and of the residue had made an abomination; so they bow themselves down to it. Know thou that their heart is ashes, and they are led astray and none can deliver his soul. Take a view of it, will you not say, "There is indeed a lie in my right hand?"

'Remember these things, O Jacob, even thou Israel, for thou art my servant. I have made thee my servant; therefore O Israel do not thou forget me. For, lo! I have made thy transgressions vanish like a cloud—and thy sins like the murky vapor. Return to me, and I will redeem thee.'"

—ALEXANDER CAMPBELL
February 10, 1831.

# Recommended Material

*Ashamed of Joseph. Mormon Foundations Crumble,* by Charles A. Crane and Steven A. Crane. College Press Publishing Company, Joplin, Missouri. ISBN: 0-89900-615-9.

*Is the Mormon My Brother? Discerning the Differences Between Mormonism and Christianity,* by James R. White. Bethany House Publishers, Minneapolis, Minnesota. ISBN: 0-7642-2047-0.

*Cults, New Religious Movements, And Your Family,* by Richard Abanes. Crossway Books, Wheaton, Illinois. ISBN: 0-89107-981-5.

*The New Mormon Challenge,* by Francis J. Beckwith, Carl Mosser and Paul Owen. Zondervan Publishers, Grand Rapids, Michigan. ISBN: 978-0-310-23194-3.

*Mormonism.* This is a 45 minute podcast by Dr. Douglas Jacoby. It's a great overview of the Mormon religion. Use the link below or search for it at www.jacobypremium.com. http://jacobypremium.com/index.php?option=com_content&view=article&id=710:mormp3&catid=63:world-religions&Itemid=81

Home | Login | Register
Currencies: US Dollar
Items: 0
Total: USD $0.00
Illumination Publishers
Lighting the Way to New Frontiers in Christian Growth
RapidSSL
Home Page
News
All Products
Specials
E-Books
Press Room
About Us
Search
THE CHRISTIAN STORY
Finding the Church in Church History
Volume 1
Dr. John M. Oakes
Gordon Ferguson
Dynamic Leadership
Principles, Roles and Relationships for a Life-Changing Church
SONGS of the KINGDOM
New Songs Volume One
River City Music Publishing
STOP
CATEGORIES
FEATURED ITEMS